Oxford Skills World

Listening

with Speaking 1

Julie Hwang

OXFORD
UNIVERSITY PRESS

OXFORD
UNIVERSITY PRESS

198 Madison Avenue
New York, NY 10016 USA

Great Clarendon Street, Oxford, OX2 6DP, United Kingdom

Oxford University Press is a department of the University of Oxford.
It furthers the University's objective of excellence in research, scholarship,
and education by publishing worldwide. Oxford is a registered trade
mark of Oxford University Press in the UK and in certain other countries

© Oxford University Press 2019

ISBN: 978 0 19 411334 2 STUDENT BOOK WITH WORKBOOK

Printed in China

This book is printed on paper from certified and well-managed sources

ACKNOWLEDGMENTS

Cover illustration and main character illustrations by: Shane McGowan/The
Organisation

Cover photograph: Peter Beavis/Getty

Back cover photograph: Oxford University Press building/David Fisher

Student Book

Illustrations by: Constanza Basaluzzo/MB Artists pp.8, 15, 22, 36, 50, 64–65, 78;
Adrian Bijloo/MB Artists pp.12–13; Hector Borlasca/MB Artists pp.9, 11, 44, 86;
Robin Boyer/Illustration Online pp.43, 85; Pascale Constantin pp.18, 27, 29;
Monique Dong/Bright Group pp.37, 39, 54–55, 72; Kevin Fales/Maggie Byers
Sprinzeles pp.79, 81; Lalena Fisher pp.30, 32; Jannie Ho/MB Artists pp.16, 25,
68–69; Anthony Lewis/MB Artists pp.46, 50–54, 56; Steffane McClary/Maggie
Byers Sprinzeles pp.23, 58; Christos Skaltsas/Advocate Art pp.40–41, 57, 67;
Laura Watson/Illustration Online pp.26, 71, 82–83

*The Publishers would like to thank the following for their kind permission to reproduce
photographs and other copyright material*: 123rf: pp.8 (monkey/wrangel), 10 (cow/
susazoom), (sheep/lightpoet), 24 (birds nest/annete), 36 (notebook/Irina
Felzina), (pen/Peerasak Kamngoen), 68 (peach/JY Lee), 70 (2b/sibyl2011), (3a/
JY Lee); Alamy: pp.38 (notebook/Panther Media GmbH), 62–63 (roller coaster/
Michael Turner), 64 (teddy bear/philipus), 68 (mango/Westend61 GmbH),
70 (4a/Westend61 GmbH); Getty: pp.6–7 (llama/olaser), 20–21 (color run/
Caiaimage/Chris Ryan), 48–49 (watermelon challenge/Malcolm MacGregor),
88 (boy playing soccer/Layland Masuda); Oxford University Press: pp.8 (sheep/
Shutterstock/1000 Words), 12 (crocodile/Shutterstock/Naypong), (elephant/
Shutterstock/Volodymyr Burdiak), (giraffe/Shutterstock), (mouse/
Shutterstock), 14 (1a/Shutterstock/Donovan van Staden), (2a/Shutterstock/
Volodymyr Burdiak), (2b/Shutterstock/CreativeNature R.Zwerver), (3a/
Shutterstock), (4a/Shutterstock), (4b/Shutterstock/Naypong), 24 (hula hoop/),
36 (eraser/Dennis Kitchen Studio, Inc), 38 (pen/Lalena Fisher), 40 (backpack/
Dennis Kitchen Studio, Inc), (ruler/Shutterstock/ScofieldZa), 42 (1b/Dennis
Kitchen Studio, Inc), (2a/Shutterstock/nikshor), (4a/Shutterstock/ScofieldZa),
64 (boat/Shutterstock/aquariagirl1970), 66 (scooter/Shutterstock/ffolas),
(teddy bear/MM Studios), 68 (carrots/Shutterstock/Olga Miltsova), 70 (2a/
Shutterstock/Olga Miltsova), (3b/Shutterstock/S-F), 78 (teeth/Shutterstock/
Paul Hakimata Photography); Shutterstock: pp.8 (cow/smereka), (duck/
Tom Middleton), 10 (duck/Gumpanat), (monkey/Patryck Kosmider), 14 (1b/
Gusdianto), (3b/Fotos593), 24 (teapot/JD_Creative Design), (game board/
Garsya), 34–35 (robot/MikeDotta), 36 (draw/Tyler Olson), 38 (hand drawing/
Julia Kuznetsova), (eraser/NuntekulPhotography), 40 (class/Syda Productions),
(paper/PannaKotta), 42 (1a/happydancing), (2b/Syda Productions), (3a/ESB
Professional), (3b/Savanevich Viktar), (4b/PannaKotta), 60 (boy outdoors
in snow/unguryanu), 64 (bike/Gena73), (scooter/Kovalchuk Oleksandr),
66 (bike/Gena73), (toy boat/bluehand), 68 (tomato/Werner Muenzker), 70 (1a/

Werner Muenzker), (1b/svf74), (4b/Tim UR), 74 (finger puppets/LukaKikina),
76–77 (climbing rock wall/Carlos Caetano), 78 (body/Monkey Business Images),
(head/iofoto), (legs/NadyaEugene), 80 (head/Anna Nahabed), (body/5 second
Studio), (teeth/Monkey Business Images), (legs/Olena Yakobchuk), 82 (eyes/
Natalia Sannikova), (face/Jaren Jai Wicklund), (mouth/wavebreakmedia),
(nose/Talita Nicolielo), 84 (1a/Jaren Jai Wicklund), (1b/Adam Jan Figel), (2a/
wavebreakmedia), (2b/schankz), (3a/Natalia Sannikova), (3b/Rob Marmion),
(4a/Talita Nicolielo), (4b/eurobanks)

Workbook

Illustrations by: Adrian Bijloo/MB Artists p.91; Hector Borlasca/MB Artists
p.107; Robin Boyer/Illustration Online pp.101, 105; Kevin Fales/Maggie Byers
Sprinzeles pp.93, 103; Jannie Ho/MB Artists p.109; Steffane McClary/Maggie
Byers Sprinzeles pp.95, 111; Christos Skaltsas/Advocate Art pp.99, 113; Laura
Watson/Illustration Online p.97

*The Publishers would like to thank the following for their kind permission to reproduce
photographs and other copyright material*: 123rf: pp.92 (1a/susazoom), (2b/
lightpoet), (3b/wrangel), (4b/susazoom), 96 (2b/Stanislau Valynkin), (3b/
annete), 100 (1a/Irina Felzina), (1b/Peerasak Kamngoen), 110 (1b/sibyl2011),
(2a/JY Lee), (3c/JY Lee); Alamy: pp.100 (3b/Panther Media GmbH), 108 (4a/
philipus), 110 (2b/Westend61 GmbH); Oxford University Press: pp.92 (3a/
Shutterstock/1000 Words), 94 (1a/Shutterstock/Volodymyr Burdiak), (1b/
Shutterstock), (1c/Shutterstock/Naypong), (2a/Shutterstock), (2b/Shutterstock/
Donovan van Staden), (2c/Shutterstock/CreativeNature R.Zwerver), (3c/
Shutterstock/Volodymyr Burdiak), 100 (3a/Dennis Kitchen Studio, Inc), (4b/
Lalena Fisher), 102 (1a/Shutterstock/ScofieldZa), (2a/Dennis Kitchen Studio,
Inc), (2c/Shutterstock/nikshor), (3a/Lalena Fisher), 108 (1b/MM Studios),
(3a/Shutterstock; aquariagirl1970), (3b/Shutterstock; ffolas), 110 (1a/
Shutterstock/S-F), (3a/Shutterstock; Olga Miltsova), 112 (2a/Shutterstock/
Paul Hakimata Photography); Shutterstock: pp.92 (2b/Tom Middleton), (2a/
Patryck Kosmider), (4a/Gumpanat), 94 (3a/Fotos593), (3b/Gusdianto), 96 (2a/
Garsya), (3a/JD_Creative Design), 100 (2a/NuntekulPhotography), (2b/Julia
Kuznetsova), (4a/Tyler Olson), 102 (1b/Savanevich Viktar), (1c/happydancing),
(2b/PannaKotta), (3b/NuntekulPhotography), (3c/PannaKotta), 108 (1a/Gena73),
(2a/Kovalchuk Oleksandr), (2b/bluehand), (4b/Gena73), 110 (1c/svf74), (2c/Tim
UR), (3b/Werner Muenzker), 112 (1a/NadyaEugene), (1b/5 second Studio), (2b/
Anna Nahabed), (4a/Olena Yakobchuk), (4b/Monkey Business Images), 114 (1a/wavebreakmedia),
(1b/Jaren Jai Wicklund), (1c/schankz), (2a/Talita Nicolielo), (2b/eurobanks), (2c/
Adam Jan Figel), (3a/Natalia Sannikova), (3b/Rob Marmion), (3c/Talita Nicolielo)

Table of Contents

TOPIC 1 **PAGE 6**

Animals Around Us

Hi! I'm Olly.

TOPIC 2 **PAGE 20**

Red Circle, Blue Square

Hi, I'm Molly!

TOPIC 3 **PAGE 34**

School Days

TOPIC 4 **PAGE 48**

Me and My Family

TOPIC 5 **PAGE 62**

Likes and Dislikes

TOPIC 6 **PAGE 76**

My Face and Body

Welcome to Oxford Skills World

Oxford Skills World: Listening with Speaking is a flexible paired skills course that takes students on a journey toward independent learning, providing them with strategies and support to reach their goals.

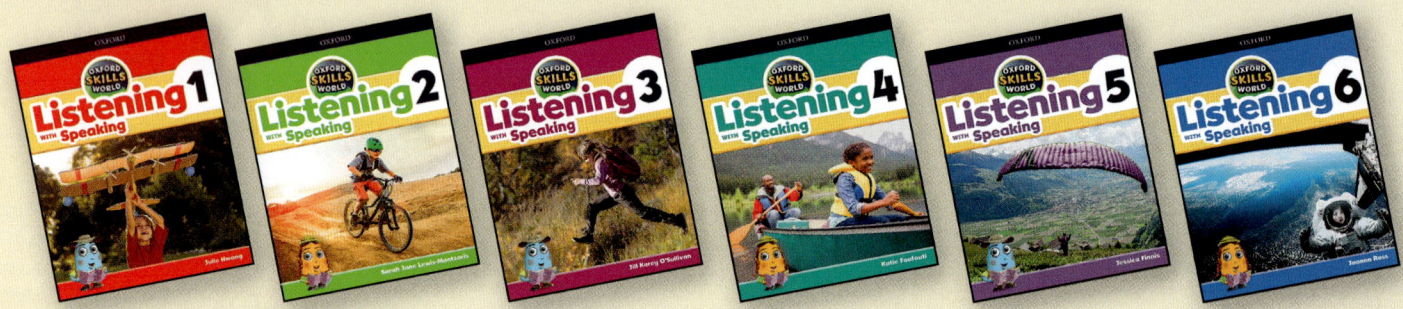

For Students

- Student Book / Workbook
- Student's website with downloadable audio and extra resources
  www.oup.com/elt/oxfordskillsworld

For Teachers

- Downloadable Teacher's Pack with instructional support, assessment, professional development videos, projects, and speaking resources
- Classroom Presentation Tool
- Teacher's website with downloadable audio and extra resources
  www.oup.com/elt/teacher/oxfordskillsworld

Be the Leader on Your Skills Adventure!

Hi! We're Olly and Molly, your skills adventure guides. We help you reach your goals by introducing new listening and speaking strategies, asking helpful questions, and giving friendly reminders. Most importantly, we cheer you on every step of the way! Let's go!

Quick Guide

Inside Each Topic

Topic Opener

Theme-based topics provide high-interest content relevant to students' lives.

My Goals introduces students to the objectives of each unit in the topic.*

Students listen to a Fun Fact to increase their engagement with the topic.

Fun characters, Olly and Molly, encourage 21st century skills like critical thinking, collaboration, and communication.

Students answer questions to activate prior knowledge and think critically.

Get Ready to Listen • Listen

Students learn and practice new vocabulary and complete the picture dictionary at the back of the book.

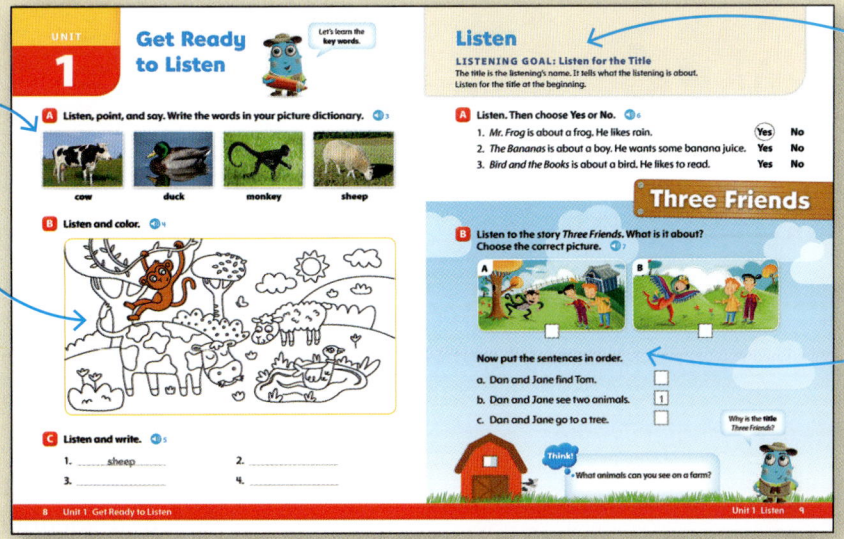

Listening Goals are strategies students can apply to any passage.

Students apply strategies to high-interest fiction and nonfiction passages, think critically about what they hear, and make connections to their own lives.

*Each topic contains two thematically related units.

Quick Guide

Understand

Students increase their comprehension of the passages by applying listening strategies they have learned.

Students complete activities to strengthen their understanding of the unit's vocabulary.

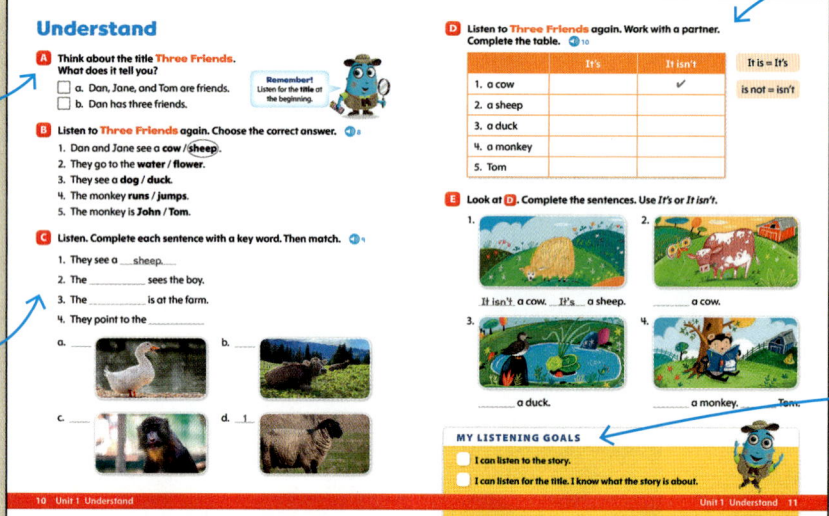

Students demonstrate comprehension of the unit's passage, vocabulary, and grammar.

At the end of each unit, students assess the progress they have made toward achieving their goals.

Listening Check

With helpful reminders from Olly and Molly, students apply the **Listening Goals** from both units to a new text.

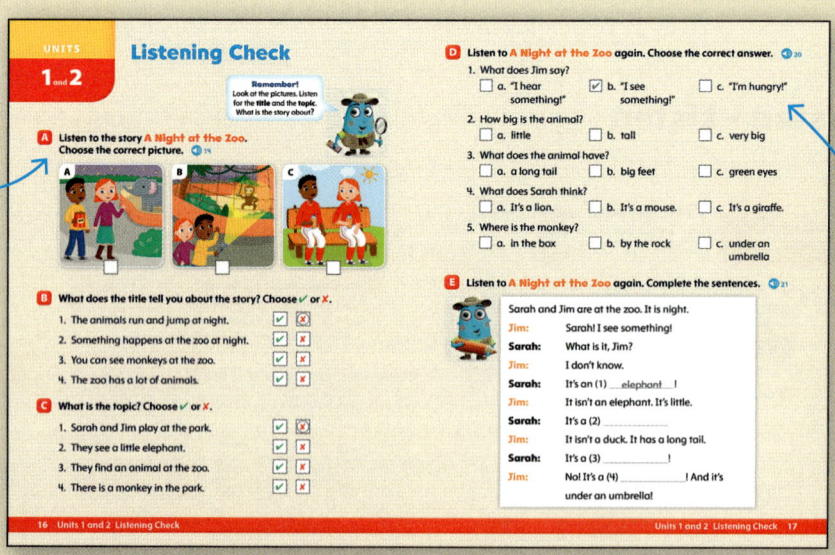

Students complete activities to boost listening comprehension and vocabulary application.

Get Ready to Speak • Speak

Speaking Goals prepare students to speak in different contexts.

Speaking Tips provide guidance on grammar, punctuation, and mechanics and help students speak fluently and accurately.

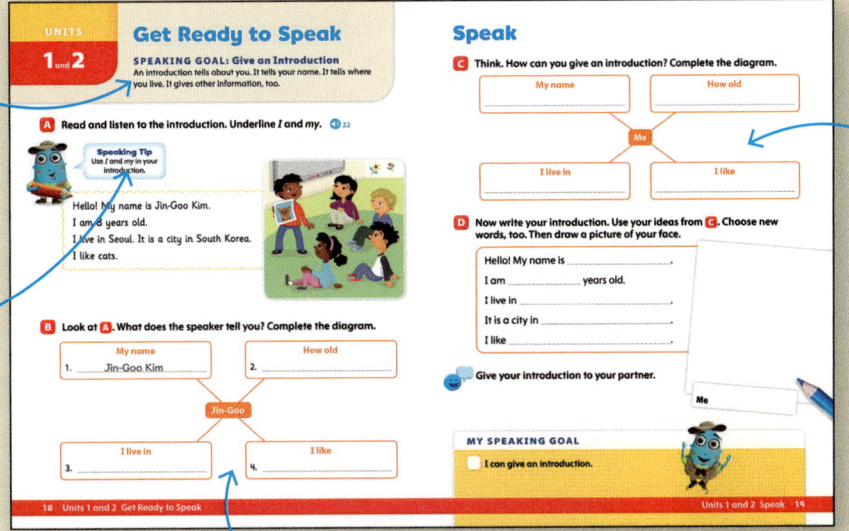

Scaffolded speaking models help students accomplish their speaking goals.

Students use graphic organizers to comprehend speaking models and to organize their thoughts for their own speaking.

Workbook

Workbook pages at the end of the book provide more opportunities for students to apply their **Listening Goals** and boost comprehension.

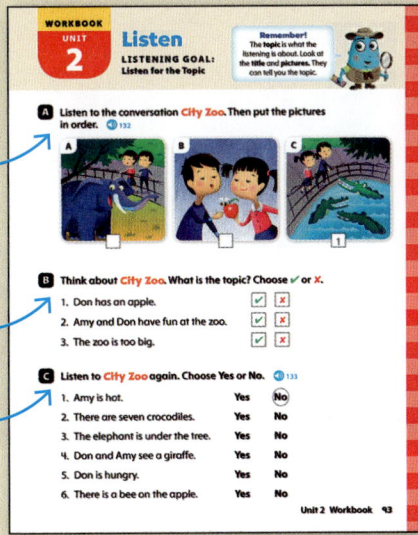

Additional activities provide extra opportunities for listening comprehension and vocabulary practice.

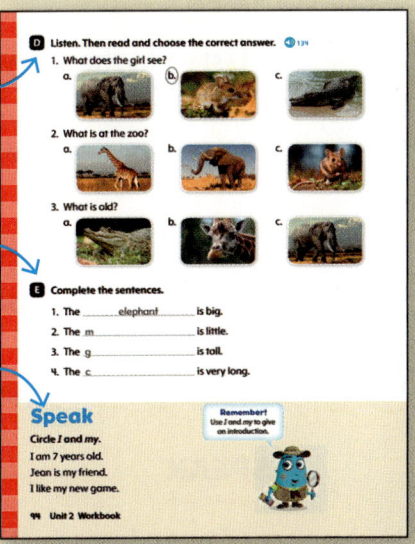

Students apply the topic's **Speaking Tip** to ensure proper usage in their own speaking.

Animals Around Us

MY GOALS

UNIT 1

- Listen to the story *Three Friends*
- Listen for the title

UNIT 2

- Listen to the passage *Animal Fun*
- Listen for the topic

SPEAK

- Give an introduction

A Look at the picture. What do you see?

1. What animals do you see?
2. Do you like the animals? Why or why not?

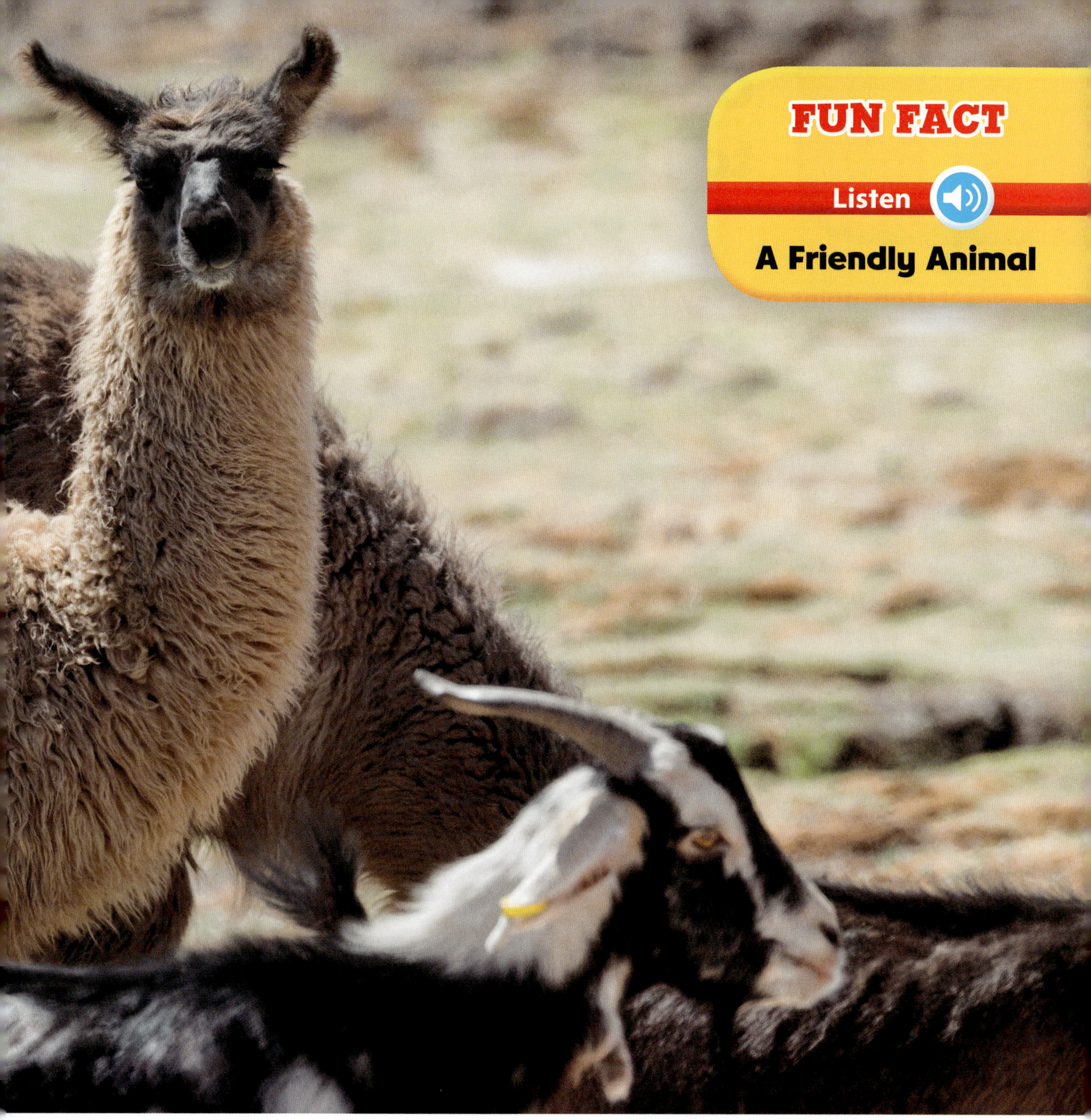

FUN FACT

Listen

A Friendly Animal

B **Listen to the Fun Fact. Then answer the questions.** 2

1. What does this animal do?
2. What is your favorite animal? Why do you like it?

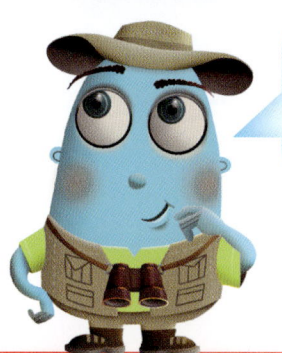

Think, Pair, Share
What animals can you see at the zoo?

Get Ready to Listen

Let's learn the **key words**.

A Listen, point, and say. Write the words in your picture dictionary. 3

cow

duck

monkey

sheep

B Listen and color. 4

C Listen and write. 5

1. ____sheep____

2. _____

3. _____

4. _____

Listen

LISTENING GOAL: Listen for the Title

The title is the listening's name. It tells what the listening is about.
Listen for the title at the beginning.

A **Listen. Then choose Yes or No.** 🔊 6

1. *Mr. Frog* is about a frog. He likes rain. **(Yes)** **No**
2. *The Bananas* is about a boy. He wants some banana juice. **Yes** **No**
3. *Bird and the Books* is about a bird. He likes to read. **Yes** **No**

Three Friends

B **Listen to the story *Three Friends*. What is it about?
Choose the correct picture.** 🔊 7

A

B

Now put the sentences in order.

a. Dan and Jane find Tom. ☐

b. Dan and Jane see two animals. **1**

c. Dan and Jane go to a tree. ☐

Why is the **title**
Three Friends?

Think!

What animals can you see on a farm?

Understand

A Think about the title **Three Friends**.
What does it tell you?

☐ a. Dan, Jane, and Tom are friends.

☐ b. Dan has three friends.

> **Remember!**
> Listen for the **title** at the beginning.

B Listen to **Three Friends** again. Choose the correct answer. 🔊 8

1. Dan and Jane see a **cow** / (**sheep**).

2. They go to the **water** / **flower**.

3. They see a **dog** / **duck**.

4. The monkey **runs** / **jumps**.

5. The monkey is **John** / **Tom**.

C Listen. Complete each sentence with a key word. Then match. 🔊 9

1. They see a _____ sheep. _____

2. The _____ sees the boy.

3. The _____ is at the farm.

4. They point to the _____

a. _____

b. _____

c. _____

d. __1__

D Listen to **Three Friends** again. Work with a partner. Complete the table. 🔊 10

	It's	It isn't
1. a cow		✔
2. a sheep		
3. a duck		
4. a monkey		
5. Tom		

It is = It's

is not = isn't

E Look at **D**. Complete the sentences. Use *It's* or *It isn't*.

1.

It isn't a cow.   It's   a sheep.

2.

_____ a cow.

3.

_____ a duck.

4.

_____ a monkey. _____ Tom.

MY LISTENING GOALS

☐ I can listen to the story.

☐ I can listen for the title. I know what the story is about.

Get Ready to Listen

Let's learn the **key words**.

A Listen, point, and say. Write the words in your picture dictionary. 11

crocodile

elephant

giraffe

mouse

B Listen and number. 🔊 12

C Listen and complete the sentences. 🔊 13

1. The _____mouse_____ eats a lot.

2. The _____ can run.

3. The _____ can kick.

4. The _____ likes bananas.

Listen

LISTENING GOAL: Listen for the Topic

The topic is what a listening is about. The title and pictures can tell you the topic.

A Listen. Choose ✔ or ✘. 14

1.
2.
3.

B Listen to the passage *Animal Fun*. What is it about? Choose the correct picture. 15

Animal Fun

A

B

Now choose ✔ or ✘.

1. The boys and girls see animals.

2. The boys and girls are in a little car.

3. The boys and girls are happy.

Where can you find the **topic**?

Think!

 Do you want to go on a safari? Why or why not?

Understand

A Think about **Animal Fun**.
What is the topic? Choose **Yes** or **No**.

1. a safari   **Yes**   **No**
2. boys and girls on a bus   **Yes**   **No**

> **Remember!**
> The **title** and **pictures** can tell you the topic.

B Listen to **Animal Fun** again. Choose the correct answer. 🔊 16

1. Where is the crocodile?
   - ☐ a. on the grass
   - ☑ b. in the water
2. Where is the giraffe?
   - ☐ a. by the water
   - ☐ b. under the tree
3. Where is the mouse?
   - ☐ a. by the bus
   - ☐ b. on the grass

C Listen and choose the correct picture. Then write the key word. 🔊 17

1. ☐ a.   ☑ b.

   giraffe

2. ☐ a.   ☐ b.

3. ☐ a.   ☐ b.

4. ☐ a.   ☐ b.

D Listen to **Animal Fun** again. Complete the diagram. 🔊 18

Where are the animals?

Crocodile	Elephant	Giraffe	Mouse
1. _in the water_	2. _____	3. _____	4. _____

E Look at **D**. Write. Use *in, on, under,* or *by.*

1.

The crocodile is ____in____ the water.

2.

The elephant is _____ the grass.

3.

The giraffe is _____ the tree.

4.

The mouse is _____ the bus.

MY LISTENING GOALS

☐ I can listen to the passage.

☐ I can listen for the topic. I know what the listening is about.

Listening Check

Remember!
Look at the pictures. Listen for the **title** and the **topic**. What is the story about?

A Listen to the story **A Night at the Zoo**. Choose the correct picture. 🔊 19

A

B

C

B What does the title tell you about the story? Choose ✔ or ✗.

1. The animals run and jump at night. ✔ ⊗
2. Something happens at the zoo at night. ✔ ✗
3. You can see monkeys at the zoo. ✔ ✗
4. The zoo has a lot of animals. ✔ ✗

C What is the topic? Choose ✔ or ✗.

1. Sarah and Jim play at the park. ✔ ⊗
2. They see a little elephant. ✔ ✗
3. They find an animal at the zoo. ✔ ✗
4. There is a monkey in the park. ✔ ✗

D Listen to **A Night at the Zoo** again. Choose the correct answer. 🔊 20

1. What does Jim say?
   - ☐ a. "I hear something!"
   - ☑ b. "I see something!"
   - ☐ c. "I'm hungry!"

2. How big is the animal?
   - ☐ a. little
   - ☐ b. tall
   - ☐ c. very big

3. What does the animal have?
   - ☐ a. a long tail
   - ☐ b. big feet
   - ☐ c. green eyes

4. What does Sarah think?
   - ☐ a. It's a lion.
   - ☐ b. It's a mouse.
   - ☐ c. It's a giraffe.

5. Where is the monkey?
   - ☐ a. in the box
   - ☐ b. by the rock
   - ☐ c. under an umbrella

E Listen to **A Night at the Zoo** again. Complete the sentences. 🔊 21

Sarah and Jim are at the zoo. It is night.

Jim: Sarah! I see something!

Sarah: What is it, Jim?

Jim: I don't know.

Sarah: It's an (1) ___elephant___!

Jim: It isn't an elephant. It's little.

Sarah: It's a (2) _____

Jim: It isn't a duck. It has a long tail.

Sarah: It's a (3) _____!

Jim: No! It's a (4) _____! And it's under an umbrella!

Get Ready to Speak

SPEAKING GOAL: Give an Introduction

An introduction tells about you. It tells your name. It tells where you live. It gives other information, too.

A Read and listen to the introduction. Underline *I* and *my*. 🔊 22

Speaking Tip
Use *I* and *my* in your introduction.

Hello! My name is Jin-Goo Kim.

I am 8 years old.

I live in Seoul. It is a city in South Korea.

I like cats.

B Look at **A**. What does the speaker tell you? Complete the diagram.

My name	How old
1. _____Jin-Goo Kim_____	2. _____

Jin-Goo

I live in	I like
3. _____	4. _____

Speak

C   Think. How can you give an introduction? Complete the diagram.

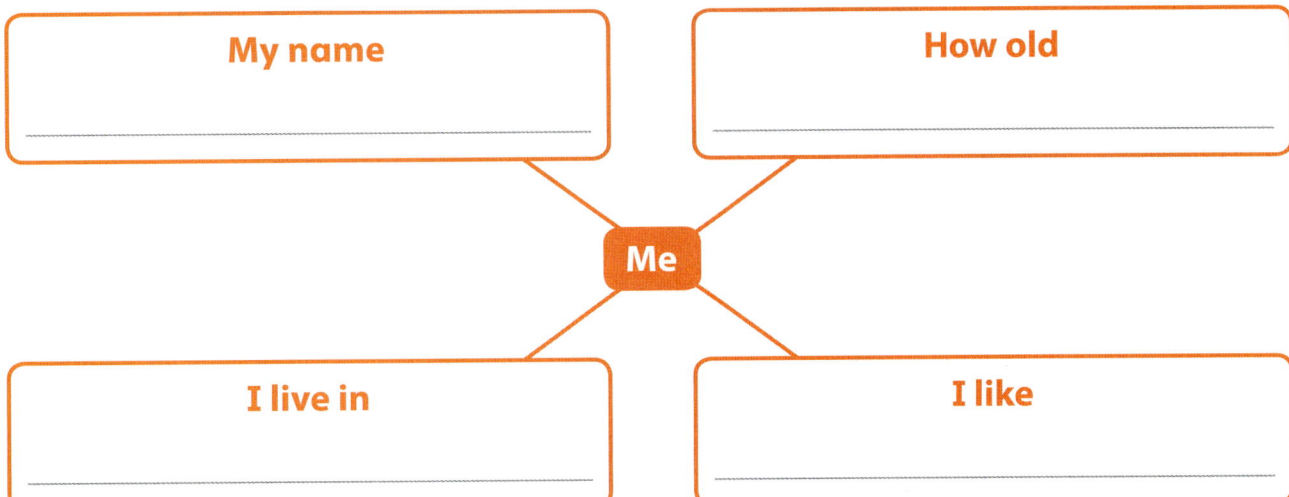

My name	How old
_____	_____

Me

I live in	I like
_____	_____

D   Now write your introduction. Use your ideas from **C**. Choose new words, too. Then draw a picture of your face.

Hello! My name is _____.

I am _____ years old.

I live in _____.

It is a city in _____.

I like _____.

Me

Give your introduction to your partner.

MY SPEAKING GOAL

☐   I can give an introduction.

TOPIC 2

ART

Red Circle, Blue Square

MY GOALS

UNIT 3

- Listen to the conversation *Cookie Count*
- Listen for numbers

UNIT 4

- Listen to the story *Fred the Clown*
- Listen for colors

SPEAK

- Give a description

A Look at the picture. What do you see?

1. How many people are there?
2. Where do you run?

FUN FACT

Listen

A Fun Run

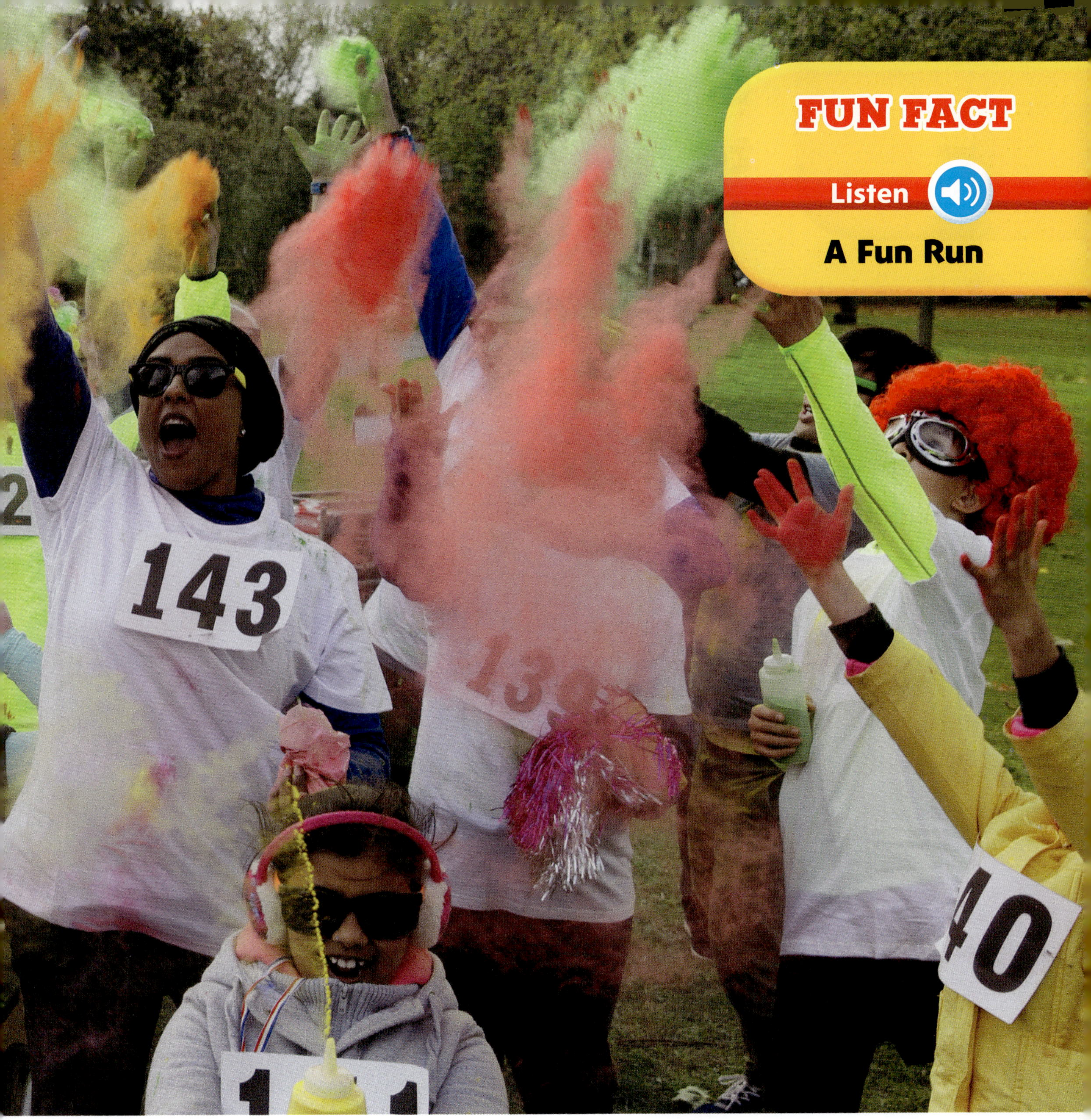

B **Listen to the Fun Fact. Then answer the questions.** 23

1. What do the people do?
2. Do you want to go on this run? Why or why not?

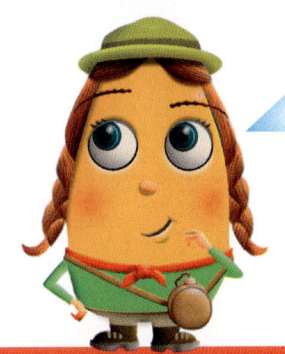

Think, Pair, Share
What colors do you like? Why? Where can you see the colors?

Get Ready to Listen

Let's learn the **key words.**

A Listen, point, and say. Write the words in your picture dictionary. 🔊 24

brown

circle

square

white

B Listen and color. 🔊 25

C Listen and write. 🔊 26

1. ___circle___

2. _____

3. _____

4. _____

Listen

LISTENING GOAL: Listen for Numbers

Words like *four* and *ten* are numbers. Numbers tell how many.

A Listen. Then complete the sentences. 🔊 27

1. She has ___three___ dolls.

2. There is _____ train.

3. There are _____ pencils.

Cookie Count

B Listen to the conversation *Cookie Count*. What is it about? Choose the correct picture. 🔊 28

A

B

Now put the sentences in order.

a. Hannah sees Oscar. ☐ 1

b. Oscar eats one cookie. ☐

c. Oscar looks at the cookies. ☐

What are the **numbers**?

Think!
• What cookies do you like?

Understand

Remember!
Numbers help us understand how many.

A Think about **Cookie Count**.
How many cookies are there?

☐ a. Oscar eats one cookie. There are seven cookies.

☐ b. Oscar eats one cookie. There are eight cookies.

B Listen to **Cookie Count** again. Choose the correct answer. 🔊 29

1. **Oscar** / **Hannah** has cookies.

2. There are **two** / **three** colors.

3. There are **white** / **purple** cookies.

4. There are **pink** / **brown** cookies.

5. There are **three** / **four** square cookies.

C Listen. Complete each sentence with a key word. Then match. 🔊 30

1. This is a ___square.___

2. The teapot is _____

3. It's a _____ nest.

4. It's a _____

a. _____

b. __1__

c. _____

d. _____

D Listen to **Cookie Count** again. Complete the diagram. 🔊 31

Cookie Count

1. Cookies
Color _____ brown _____
Shape _____

2. Cookies
Color _____
Shape _____

E Look at **D**. Complete the sentences. Use *this*, *is*, *brown*, or *white*.

1.

Is __this__ a circle?

Yes, it is. It's a circle.

2.

Is _____ a circle?

No, it isn't. It's a square.

3.

_____ this a white circle?

No, it isn't. It's a _____ circle.

4.

Is _____ a brown square?

No, it isn't. It's a _____ square.

MY LISTENING GOALS

☐ I can listen to the conversation.

☐ I can listen for numbers. Numbers tell how many.

Get Ready to Listen

Let's learn the **key words**.

A Listen, point, and say. Write the words in your picture dictionary. 🔊 32

blue

green

red

yellow

B Listen and number. 🔊 33

C Listen and complete the sentences. 🔊 34

1. The pencil is ___green.___

2. He has a _____ vest.

3. She is in the _____ car.

4. I have a _____ yo-yo.

Listen

LISTENING GOAL: Listen for Colors

Words like *red* and *blue* are colors. Listen for color words. They tell what color things are.

A Listen. Choose ✔ or ✘. 🔊 35

1.
2.
3.

Fred the Clown

B Listen to the story *Fred the Clown*. What is it about?
Choose the correct picture. 🔊 36

Now choose ✔ or ✘.

1. Fred doesn't have the car.

2. Fred sees Joe.

3. Joe has Fred's guitar.

What **color** is Fred's car?

Think!
- What colors are your toys? What colors are your friends' toys?

Understand

Remember!
Color words tell what color things are.

A Think about **Fred the Clown**.
What color words are in the story? Choose **Yes** or **No**.

1. black, orange, pink, purple   **Yes**   **No**
2. red, yellow, green, blue   **Yes**   **No**

B Listen to **Fred the Clown** again. Choose the correct answer. 37

1. Who has Fred's car?
   - ☑ a. Joe   ☐ b. Jim
2. What color is Fred's skateboard?
   - ☐ a. orange   ☐ b. red
3. What color is Fred's balloon?
   - ☐ a. blue   ☐ b. purple

C Listen and choose the correct picture. Then write the key word. 38

1.

☐ a.   ☑ b.

green

2.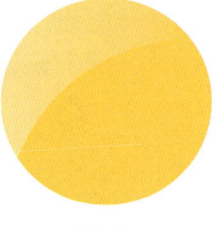

☐ a.   ☐ b.

3.

☐ a.   ☐ b.

4.

☐ a.   ☐ b.

D Listen to **Fred the Clown** again. Work with a partner. Complete the diagram. 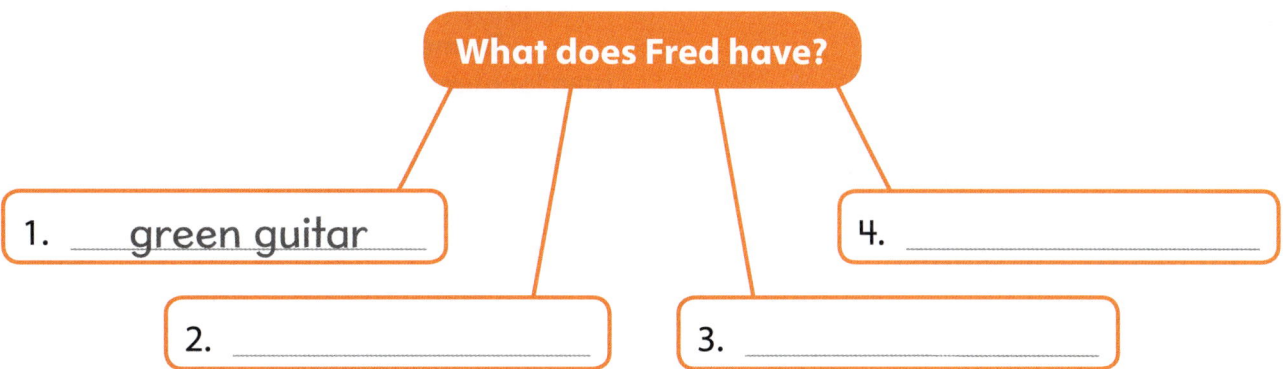 39

What does Fred have?

1. _____green guitar_____

4. _____

2. _____

3. _____

E Look at **D**. Write. Use *have, has,* or *don't have.*

1.

He ____has____ a green guitar.

2.

He _____ a red skateboard.

3.

I _____ an orange balloon.

I _____ a blue balloon.

4.

I _____ my car.

You _____ my yellow car!

MY LISTENING GOALS

☐ I can listen to the story.

☐ I can listen for color words. They tell what color things are.

Listening Check

A Listen to the poem **Traffic Light**. Choose the correct picture. 🔊 40

A

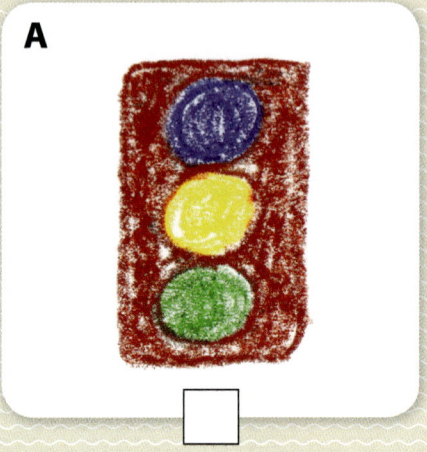

☐

B

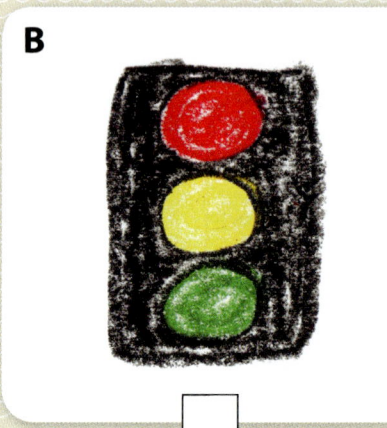

☐

C

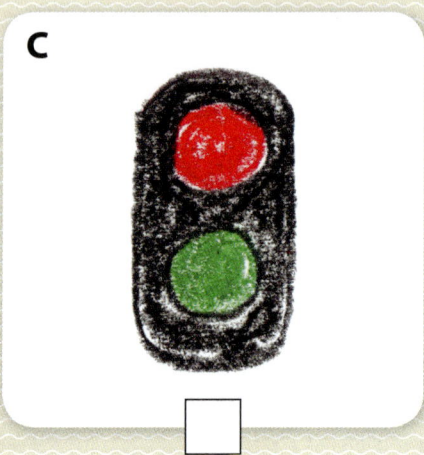

☐

B Read the sentences. Are the numbers correct? Choose ✔ or ✘.

1. There are two circles. ✔ ⊗

2. There is one red circle. ✔ ✘

3. There is one black box. ✔ ✘

4. There are three squares. ✔ ✘

C Read the sentences. Are the colors correct? Choose ✔ or ✘.

1. There is one green circle. ✔ ✘

2. Yellow says "slow." ✔ ✘

3. There is one black circle. ✔ ✘

4. Green says "stop." ✔ ✘

D Listen to **Traffic Light** again. Choose the correct answer. 🔊 41

1. What shape is green?
   ☐ a. a square   ☑ b. a circle   ☐ c. a rectangle

2. What does red say?
   ☐ a. go   ☐ b. slow   ☐ c. stop

3. How many yellow circles are there?
   ☐ a. one   ☐ b. two   ☐ c. three

4. How many colors are there?
   ☐ a. three   ☐ b. four   ☐ c. five

5. What is in the poem?
   ☐ a. a pen   ☐ b. crayons   ☐ c. a pencil

E Listen to **Traffic Light** again. Complete the sentences. 🔊 42

I draw three (1) ____circles____

One, two, three

I see circles.

Red, (2) _____, green

I have (3) _____

Red says "stop!"

I have yellow.

Yellow says "slow."

I have green.

(4) _____ says "go!"

One black box. I have black.

This is a traffic light.

Go, crayons, go!

Vrooom!

Get Ready to Speak

SPEAKING GOAL: Give a Description

A description tells what something looks like. It can be about people, places, or things.

A Read and listen to the description. What words tell about the tree? What words tell about the sun? Circle the words. 🔊 43

Speaking Tip
Use color and shape words in your description.

The Park

This is a tree. It's big.

It's green and brown.

This is the sun. It's a circle.

It's yellow.

B Look at **A**. What does the speaker say? Use the words from the description. Complete the diagram.

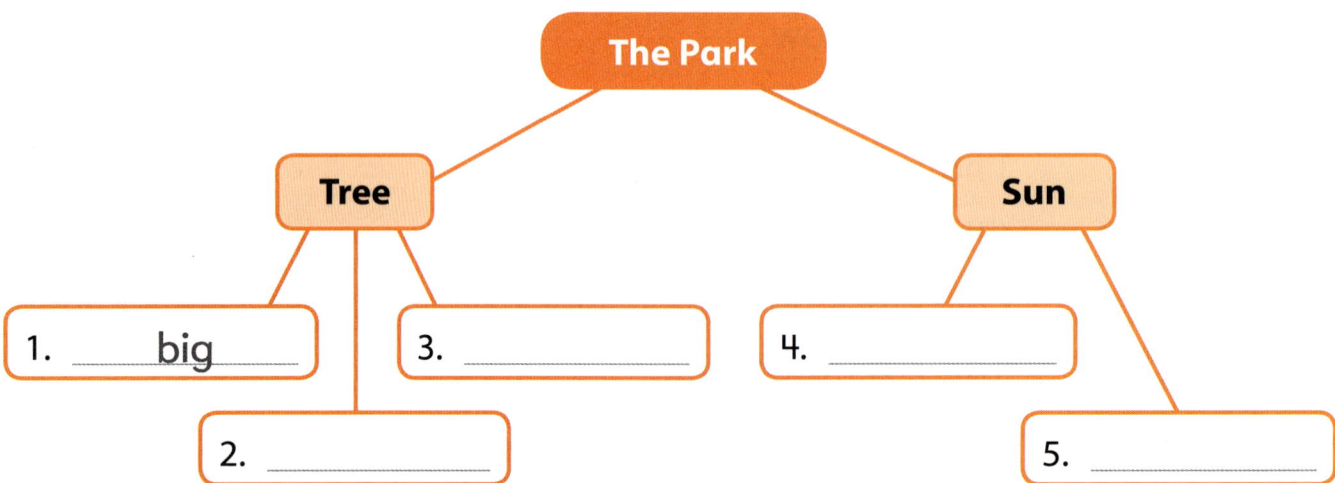

The Park

Tree — Sun

1. ____big____   3. _____   4. _____

2. _____   5. _____

Speak

C Think about a favorite place. What words tell about the place? Complete the diagram.

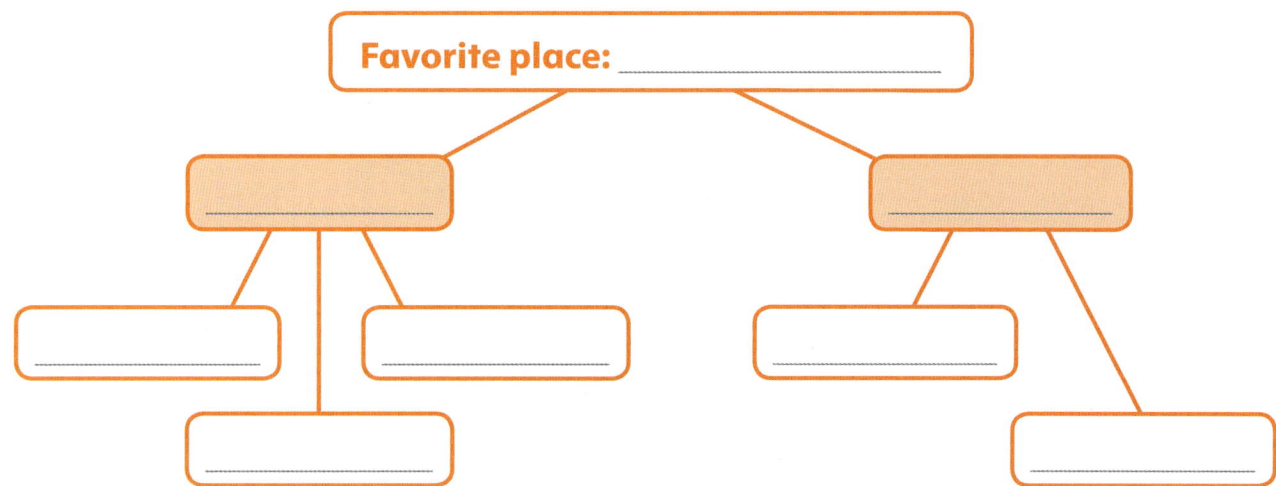

Favorite place: _____

D Now write your description. Use your ideas from **C**. Choose new words, too. Then draw a picture of the place.

This is _____.

It's _____.

It's _____ and _____.

This is _____.

It's _____.

It's _____.

Give your description to your partner. Use your picture.

TOPIC 3

SOCIAL STUDIES

School Days

MY GOALS

UNIT 5

- Listen to the story *The Special Notebook*
- Listen for greetings and endings

UNIT 6

- Listen to the conversation *The Box*
- Listen for key words

SPEAK

- Use greetings and endings

 A **Look at the picture. What do you see?**

1. Where are the children?
2. Do you like robots? Why or why not?

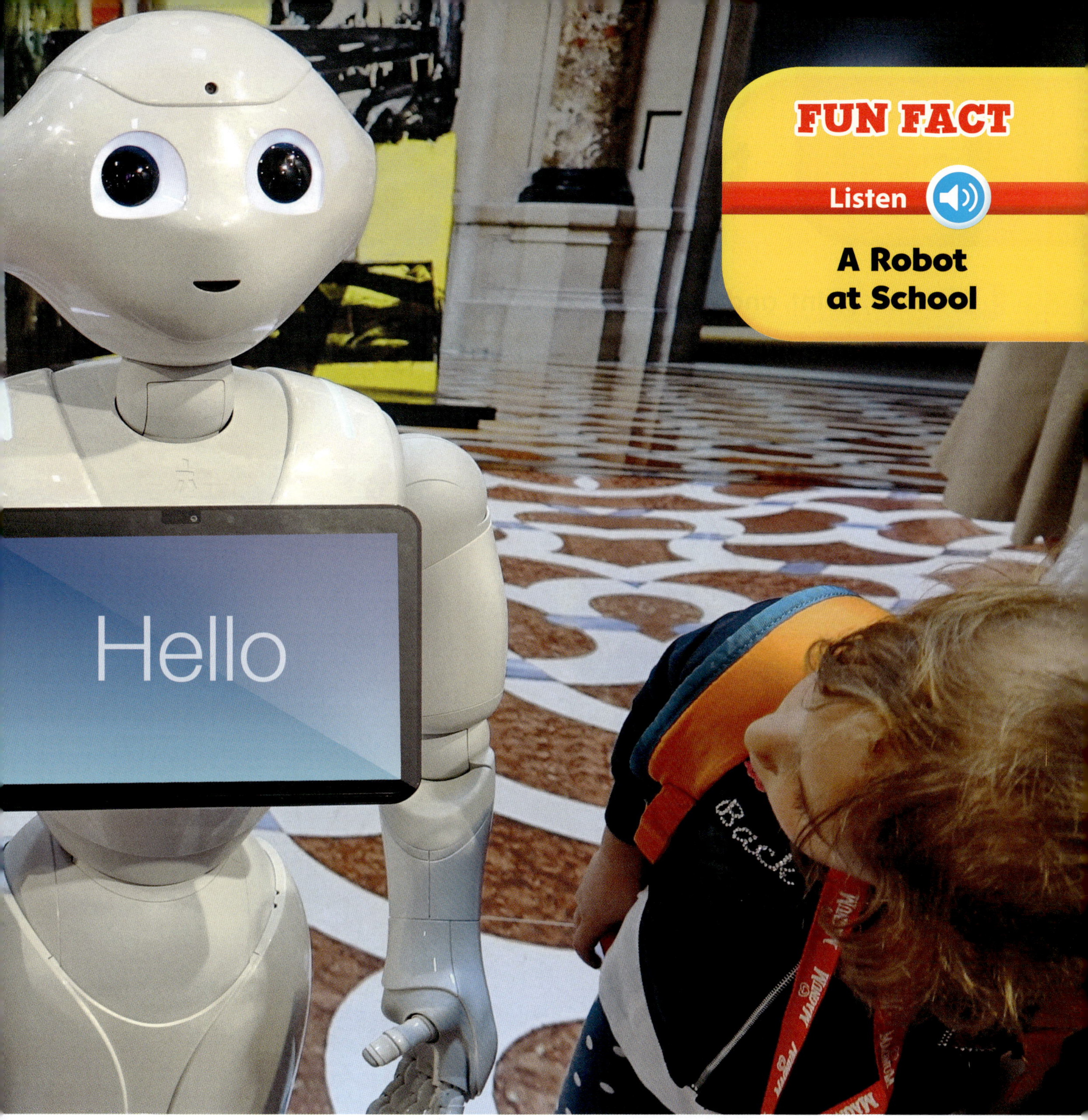

Hello

B **Listen to the Fun Fact. Then answer the questions.** 🔊 44

1. What can the robot do?

2. Can a robot help you at school? What can it do?

Think, Pair, Share
What things do you have at your school?

Get Ready to Listen

Let's learn the **key words**.

A Listen, point, and say. Write the words in your picture dictionary.  45

draw

eraser

notebook

pen

B Listen and color. 46

C Listen and write. 47

1. ___notebook___

2. _____

3. _____

4. _____

Listen

Greetings start a conversation. They are words like *hello* or *hi*. Endings stop a conversation. They are words like *goodbye* or *see you later*.

A **Listen. Then complete the sentences.** 🔊 48

1. The greeting is _____ hi. _____

2. The ending is _____

3. The teacher says _____ to Kayo.

The Special Notebook

B **Listen to the story *The Special Notebook*. What is it about? Choose the correct picture.** 🔊 49

A

B

Now put the sentences in order.

a. Mei and Paul go to the zoo. ☐

b. Paul uses the eraser. ☐

c. Paul draws a picture. 1

What does Paul say at the **end**?

Think!

• Where do you want to go?

Understand

A Think about **The Special Notebook**. What is the greeting? What are the endings? Choose the correct answer.

☐ a. hello, we're home, and goodbye

☐ b. hi, see you later, and goodbye

Remember!
Greetings start a conversation. **Endings** stop a conversation.

B Listen to **The Special Notebook** again. Choose the correct answer. 🔊 50

1. Paul has a **crayon** / **notebook**.

2. He draws a **beach** / **zoo**.

3. Paul and Mei see a **lion** / **crocodile**.

4. Paul has **a book bag** / **an eraser**.

5. Mei **likes** / **doesn't like** the notebook.

C Listen. Complete each sentence with a key word. Then match. 🔊 51

1. This is my _____pen._____

2. The _____ is little.

3. I _____ at the table.

4. It's my _____

a. _____

b. __1__

c. _____

d. _____

D Listen to **The Special Notebook** again. Work with a partner. Complete the diagram. 🔊 52

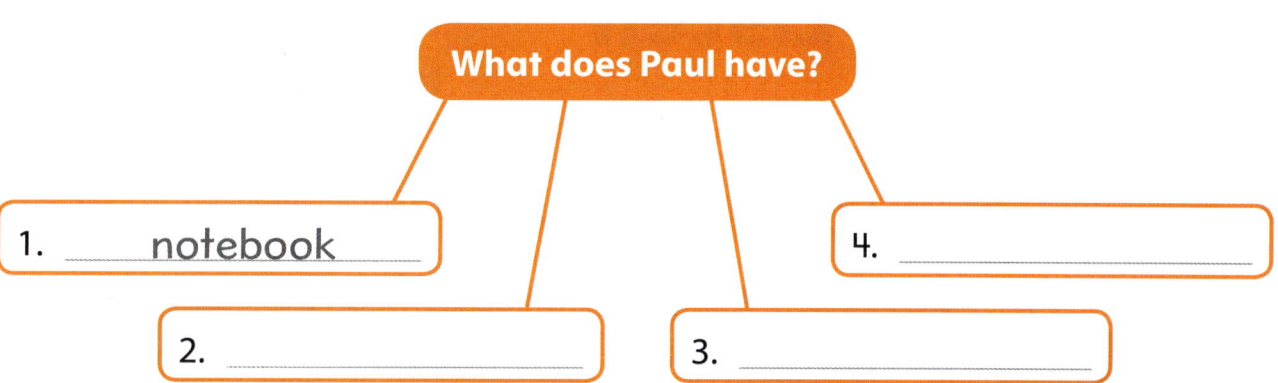

What does Paul have?

1. _____notebook_____

2. _____

3. _____

4. _____

E Look at **D**. Complete the sentences. Use *is*, *this*, or *my*.

1.

This _____is_____ my notebook.

2.

This is _____ pen.

3.

This _____ my pencil.

4.

_____ is my eraser.

MY LISTENING GOALS

☐ I can listen to the story.

☐ I can listen for greetings and endings. They start and stop a conversation.

Get Ready to Listen

Let's learn the **key words**.

A Listen, point, and say. Write the words in your picture dictionary. 53

backpack

class

paper

ruler

B Listen and number. 🔊 54

C Listen and complete the sentences. 🔊 55

1. The ____paper____ is in the cupboard.

2. This is my _____

3. It's a _____

4. I have a big _____

Listen

LISTENING GOAL: Listen for Key Words

Key words are words you hear many times. Key words tell what a listening is about.

A Listen. Choose the correct answer.  56

1. The key word is **pencil** / **long**.
2. The key word is **notebook** / **book**.
3. The key word is **table** / **flower**.

The Box

B Listen to the conversation *The Box*. What is it about?
Choose the correct picture. 57

A

B

Now choose ✔ or ✘.

1. There are two people.　　　✔　✘

2. The boy talks to his aunt.　　✔　✘

3. The boy talks with his mom.　✔　✘

What words do they say **many times**?

Think!

• What present do you want? Why?

Understand

Remember!
You hear **key words** many times.

A Think about **The Box**. What are the key words? Choose **Yes** or **No**.

1. *box* and *class*   **Yes**   **No**
2. *present* and *backpack*   **Yes**   **No**

B Listen to **The Box** again. Choose the correct answer.  58

1. Who gives a present to the boy?
   ☐ a. his teacher   ✔ b. his mom
2. What is in the box?
   ☐ a. a backpack   ☐ b. a ruler
3. Where can he take the present?
   ☐ a. to class   ☐ b. to the store

C Listen and choose the correct picture. Then write the key word. 59

1.

   ☐ a.   ✔ b.

   backpack

2.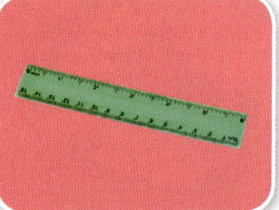

   ☐ a.   ☐ b.

3.

   ☐ a.   ☐ b.

4.

   ☐ a.   ☐ b.

D Listen to **The Box** again. What are some questions? Work with a partner. Complete the diagram. 🔊 60

1. _____What's_____ in the box?

2. _____ a ruler?

Questions

3. _____ paper?

4. _____ a backpack?

E Look at **D**. Write. Use *is*, *it*, or *isn't*.

1.

What's in the box?

_____It_____'s a present.

2.

_____ it a ruler?

No, it isn't.

3.

Is it paper?

No, it _____ .

4.

Is _____ a backpack?

Yes, _____ is!

MY LISTENING GOALS

☐ I can listen to the conversation.

☐ I can listen for key words. They tell what the listening is about.

Listening Check

A Listen to the story **Mouse and Frog**.
Choose the correct picture. 🔊 61

A

B

C

B What is the greeting in the story? What is the ending? Choose ✔ or ✘.

1. hi   ✔   ✘
2. hello   ✔   ✘
3. goodbye   ✔   ✘
4. see you later ✔   ✘

C What are the key words? Choose ✔ or ✘.

1. pen   ✔   ✘
2. backpack   ✔   ✘
3. paper   ✔   ✘
4. eraser   ✔   ✘

D Listen to **Mouse and Frog** again. Choose the correct answer. 🔊 62

1. Who has a backpack?
   ☐ a. Frog   ☑ b. Mouse   ☐ c. Bird

2. What does Mouse have?
   ☐ a. a ruler   ☐ b. a pencil   ☐ c. a pen

3. Where is the paper?
   ☐ a. in the desk   ☐ b. at home   ☐ c. in the backpack

4. What does Mouse do?
   ☐ a. He jumps.   ☐ b. He dances.   ☐ c. He eats.

5. Who finds the eraser?
   ☐ a. Frog   ☐ b. Mouse   ☐ c. the teacher

E Listen to **Mouse and Frog** again. Complete the sentences. 🔊 63

"Hello, Mouse!" says Frog.

"Hello, Frog! Look in my (1) __backpack__!

I have a pen and (2) _____.

And this is my eraser."

Mouse is happy. He jumps.

The (3) _____ and eraser jump, too.

"Where are my pen and eraser?"

"This is your pen.

This is your (4) _____!" says Frog.

"Thank you!"

"See you later!" says Frog.

Get Ready to Speak

SPEAKING GOAL: Use Greetings and Endings

A conversation is a talk with two or more people. Conversations have greetings and endings.

A Read and listen to the conversation. Underline the greetings. Underline the endings. 🔊 64

> **Speaking Tip**
> Use words like *hello* or *hi* to start a conversation.
> Use words like *goodbye* or *see you later* to end it.

Trang: Hello, Mark.

Mark: Hi, Trang!

Trang: Look! I have a doll in my backpack!

Mark: It's a nice doll!

Trang: Thank you. See you later!

Mark: Goodbye, Trang!

B Look at **A**. What are the greetings? What are the endings? Complete the diagram.

1. _____ hello _____

2. _____

Greetings and Endings

3. _____

4. _____

Speak

C Think about your conversations. What greetings do you use?
What endings do you use? Complete the diagram.

```
┌─────────────────────────┐        ┌─────────────────────────┐
│ _____    │        │ _____    │
└─────────────────────────┘        └─────────────────────────┘
              ╲              ╱
          ┌──────────────────────────┐
          │  Greetings and Endings   │
          └──────────────────────────┘
              ╱              ╲
┌─────────────────────────┐        ┌─────────────────────────┐
│ _____    │        │ _____    │
└─────────────────────────┘        └─────────────────────────┘
```

D Now work with your partner. Write a conversation about a backpack.
What's in it? Use your greetings and endings from **C**.
Then draw the things in the backpack.

> **Me:** _____, _____.
>
> **My partner:** _____, _____!
>
> **Me:** Look! I have a(n) _____
> in my backpack!
>
> **My partner:** It's a nice _____!
>
> **Me:** _____. _____!
>
> **My partner:** _____, _____!

Say your conversation with your partner.

MY SPEAKING GOAL

☐ I can use greetings. I can use endings.

TOPIC 4

SOCIAL STUDIES

Me and My Family

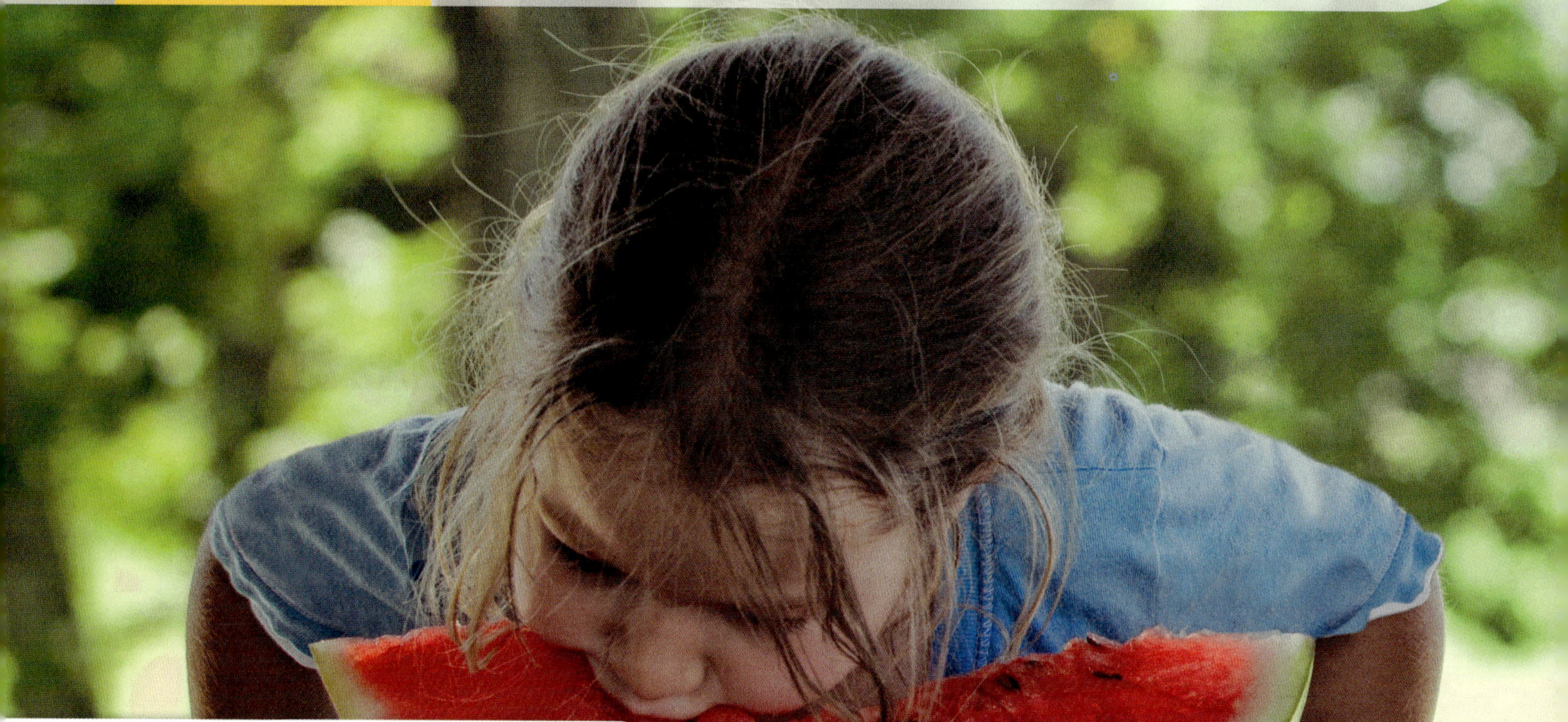

MY GOALS

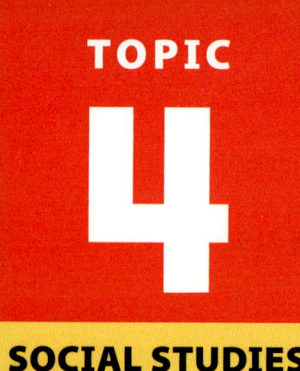

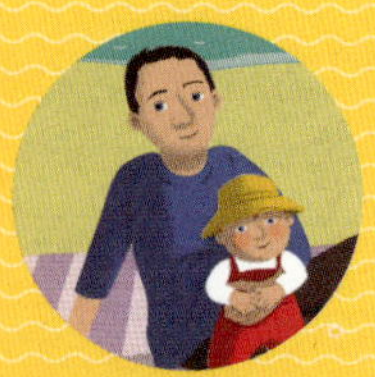

UNIT 7

- Listen to the story *My Family*
- Listen for questions

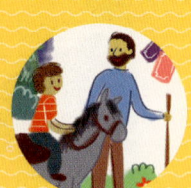

UNIT 8

- Listen to the presentation *My Summer*
- Listen for answers

SPEAK

- Ask questions to find information

A **Look at the picture. What do you see?**

1. What's funny about this picture?
2. Do you like watermelon? What's your favorite fruit?

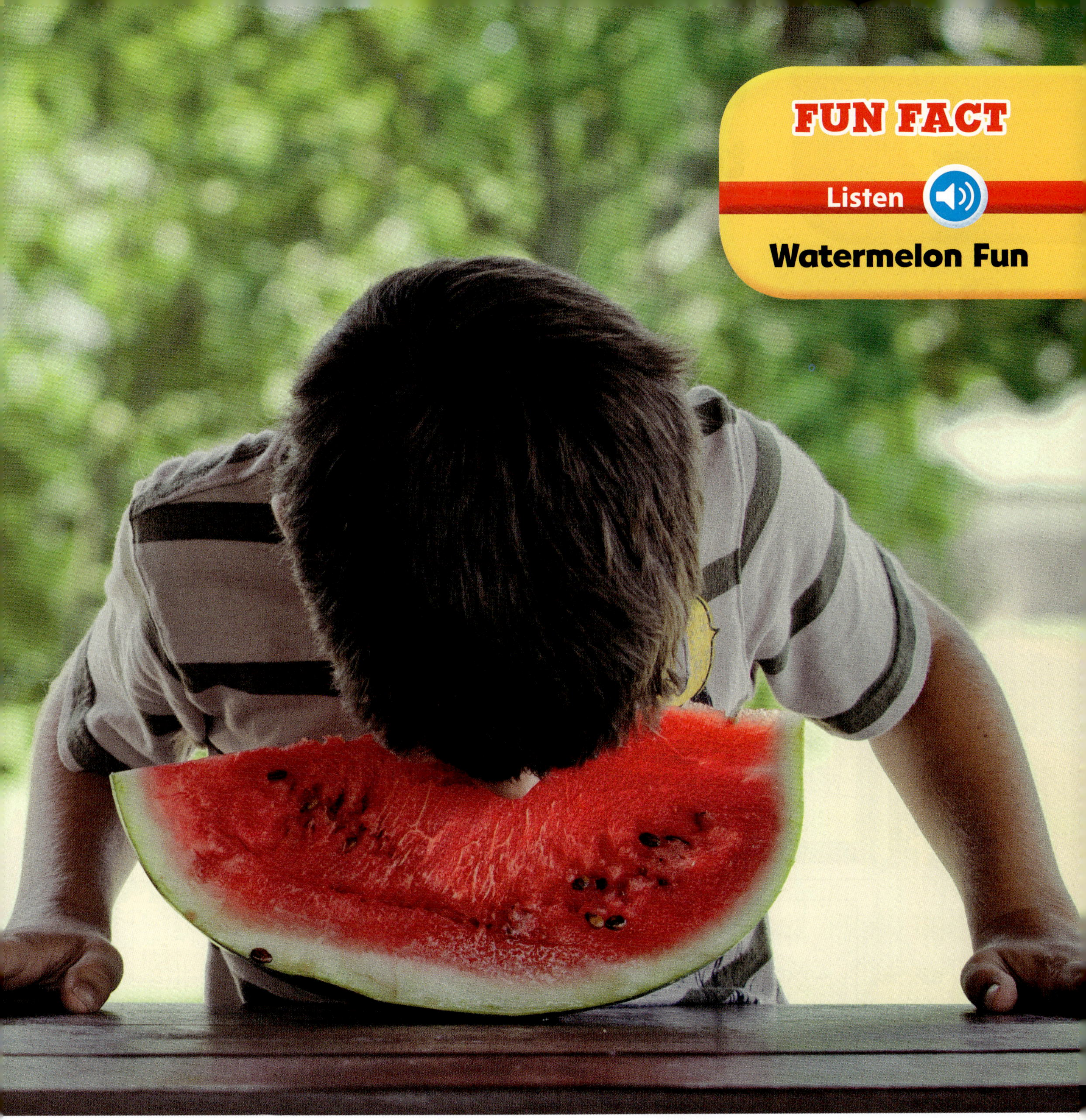

FUN FACT

Listen

Watermelon Fun

B **Listen to the Fun Fact. Then answer the questions.** 65

1. Do they eat fast or slow? Do they eat a little or a lot?
2. What games do you like?

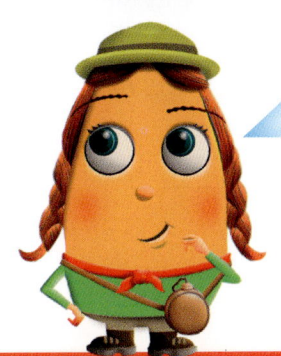

Think, Pair, Share
What games do you play with your family?

Get Ready to Listen

Let's learn the **key words**.

A Listen, point, and say. Write the words in your picture dictionary. 66

parents

boy

girl

children

B Listen and color. 67

C Listen and write. 68

1. _____girl_____   2. _____

3. _____   4. _____

Listen

Questions ask for information. They begin with words like *what*, *where*, or *who*. Listen for these words.

A **Listen. Then complete the sentences.** 🔊 69

1. The question word is _____who._____

2. The question word is _____

3. The question word is _____

My Family

B **Listen to the story *My Family*. What is it about? Choose the correct picture.** 🔊 70

A

B

Now choose ✔ or ✘.

1. Meg looks at a picture.   ✅ ✘

2. The picture shows Rosa's family.   ✔ ✘

3. The family has four children.   ✔ ✘

What are the **question words**?

Think!

• Where do you go with your family?

Understand

A Think about **My Family**.
What question is in the story?

☐ a. Where is the boy?

☐ b. Who are they?

> **Remember!**
> **Questions** ask
> for information.

B Listen to **My Family** again. Choose the correct answer. 🔊 71

1. The picture shows (**Matt's**) / **Meg's** parents.
2. They are at the **beach** / **playground**.
3. The boy's name is **Jason** / **Jack**.
4. Jessie is a **boy** / **girl**.
5. Matt **likes** / **doesn't like** fish.

C Listen. Complete each sentence with a key word. Then match. 🔊 72

1. My ___parents___ are at the beach.

2. I can see the _____

3. The _____ has a cup.

4. The _____ has a cup, too.

a. _____

b. _1_

c. _____

d. _____

D Listen to **My Family** again. What are the questions? Complete the diagram. 🔊 73

1. ___Who___
   are they?

2. _____
   is this?

Questions

3. _____
   are the children?

4. _____
   is this?

E Look at **D**. Write the questions. Use *who*, *where*, or *what*.

1.

___Who are they?___
They are my parents.

2.

_____
This is the beach.

3.

_____
They are Jason and Jessie.

4.

_____
It's fish.

MY LISTENING GOALS

☐ I can listen to the story.

☐ I can listen for questions.

Get Ready to Listen

Let's learn the **key words**.

A Listen, point, and say. Write the words in your picture dictionary. 74

grandparents

uncle

cousin

family

B Listen and number. 🔊 75

C Listen and complete the sentences. 🔊 76

1. My ___grandparents___ are at home.

2. The teacher talks to my _____

3. My _____ likes pizza.

4. My _____ is in my class.

Listen

LISTENING GOAL: Listen for Answers

We say answers after questions. Answers give information. Listen to the questions. Then listen to what comes next.

A Listen. Does the picture show the answer? Choose ✔ or ✘. 🔊 77

1.
2.
3.

B Listen to the presentation *My Summer*. What is it about? Choose the correct picture. 🔊 78

My Summer

A

B

Now put the sentences in order.

a. The family goes to the grandparents' house. `1`

b. The boy and his uncle ride bicycles.

c. They play a game.

What do we get from **answers**?

Think!

What do you do in the summer?

Understand

A Think about **My Summer**. What answer is in the presentation? Choose **Yes** or **No**.

1. He's my uncle.   **Yes**   **No**
2. These are my parents.   **Yes**   **No**

> **Remember!**
> Listen for an **answer** *after* a question.

B Listen to **My Summer** again. Choose the correct answer. 🔊 79

1. What is in the picture?
   - ✔ a. the grandparents' house
   - ☐ b. the parents' house
2. What does the boy do?
   - ☐ a. He plays a game.
   - ☐ b. He swims.
3. Who is tall?
   - ☐ a. the cousin
   - ☐ b. the uncle

C Listen and choose the correct picture. Then write the key word. 🔊 80

1.
   ☐ a.   ✔ b.

   grandparents

2.
   ☐ a.   ☐ b.

3.
   ☐ a.   ☐ b.

4.
   ☐ a.   ☐ b.

D Listen to **My Summer** again. What word tells about each person or thing? Work with a partner. Complete the diagram. 🔊 81

My Summer

House
1. It's _____big._____

Game
2. It's _____

Uncle
3. He's _____

Cousin
4. She's _____

E Look at **D**. Write sentences. Use *he's, she's, or it's.*

1.

This is my grandparents' house.

_____It's big._____

2.

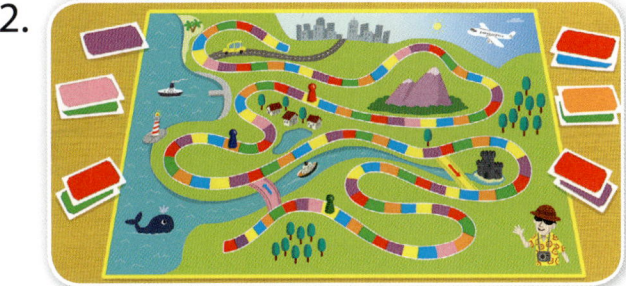

This is a game.

_____

3.

This is my uncle.

_____

4.

This is my cousin.

_____

MY LISTENING GOALS

☐ I can listen to the conversation.

☐ I can listen for answers.

Listening Check

Remember!
Listen for **questions**. What do they ask? Listen for **answers**. What do they tell you?

A **Listen to the conversation Apple Farm. Choose the correct picture.** 🔊 82

A

B

C

B **What questions are in the conversation? Choose ✔ or ✘.**

1. Who is John? ✅ ✘

2. Is he tall? ✔ ✘

3. Where are your parents? ✔ ✘

4. Do you have apples? ✔ ✘

C **What answers are in the conversation? Choose ✔ or ✘.**

1. He's my brother. ✔ ⊗

2. No, he isn't. He's short. ✔ ✘

3. Yes, he is. He has a blue cap. ✔ ✘

4. Yes, I have 10 apples! ✔ ✘

Listen to Apple Farm again. Choose the correct answer. 🔊 83

1. How many boys are there?
   ☐ a. two   ☑ b. three   ☐ c. four

2. Who is John?
   ☐ a. a cousin   ☐ b. an uncle   ☐ c. a parent

3. What does John have?
   ☐ a. a red shirt   ☐ b. a blue car   ☐ c. a blue cap

4. Where is John?
   ☐ a. under the tree   ☐ b. on the chair   ☐ c. by the table

5. How many apples are there?
   ☐ a. 12   ☐ b. 20   ☐ c. 10

E **Listen to Apple Farm again. Complete the sentences.** 🔊 84

Three (1) _____boys_____ are at an apple farm.

Chris: Where is John?

Todd: Who is John?

Chris: He's my (2) _____

Todd: There are some (3) _____. I see a boy.

Is he tall?

Chris: Yes, he is. He has a blue cap.

Todd: He's with your (4) _____!

He's under the tree.

Chris: John! Do you have apples?

Todd: Yes, I have 10 apples!

Get Ready to Speak

SPEAKING GOAL:
Ask Questions to Find Information
Questions help you get information. They help you find out about a person, place, or thing.

A Read and listen to the conversation. Underline the question words. 85

Speaking Tip
Use question words like *who*, *what*, or *how* to find information.

Lily: Who is this?

Justin: This is my cousin.

Lily: Where does he live?

Justin: He lives in Canada.

Lily: How old is he?

Justin: He's 11 years old.

B Look at **A**. What are the questions? Complete the diagram.

My Cousin

Questions	Answers
1. Who is this? →	This is my cousin.
2. _____ →	He lives in Canada.
3. _____ →	He's 11 years old.

Speak

C Think about someone in your family. Complete the diagram.

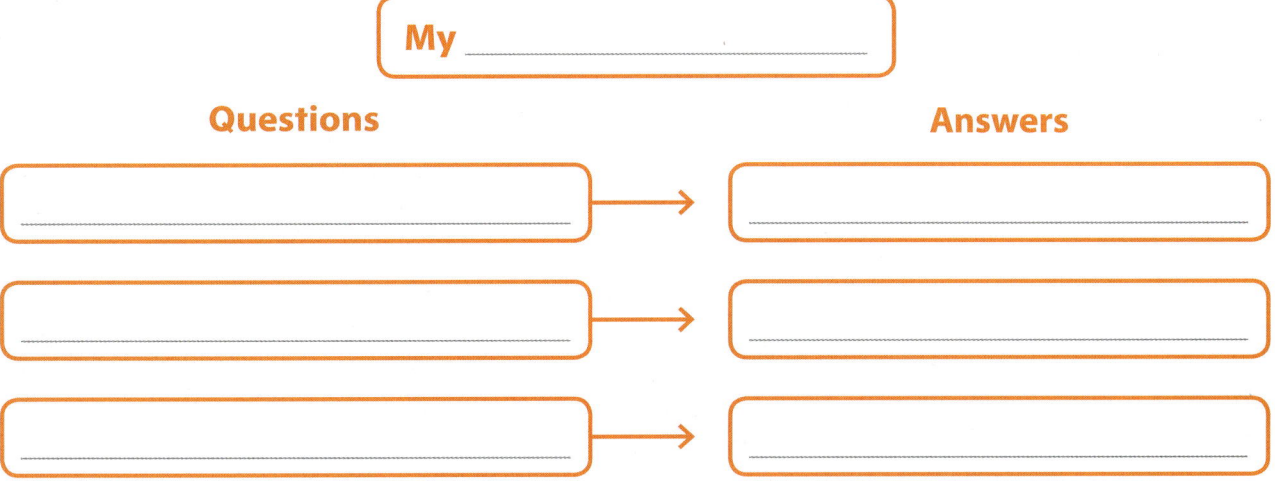

My _____

Questions

Answers

_____	→	_____
_____	→	_____
_____	→	_____

D Draw the person. Then write about the person. Use your ideas from **C**. Choose new words, too.

This is my _____.

He / She _____.

He's / She's _____.

Look at your partner's picture. Then ask questions about your partner's picture. What do you find out about the person?

MY SPEAKING GOAL

☐ I can ask questions to find information.

TOPIC 5

SOCIAL STUDIES

Likes and Dislikes

MY GOALS

UNIT 9

- Listen to the story *Teddy Bear and Bird*
- Listen for likes

UNIT 10

- Listen to the passage *Pete and Mia*
- Listen for dislikes

SPEAK

- Describe likes and dislikes

A Look at the picture. What do you see?

1. Are the people happy or sad?
2. Where do you go for fun?

B **Listen to the Fun Fact. Then answer the questions.** 🔊 86

1. Is it long or short? Is it fast or slow?

2. Can you ride a roller coaster?
Do you like it? Why or why not?

Think, Pair, Share
What do you like to ride?

Get Ready to Listen

Let's learn the **key words**.

A Listen, point, and say. Write the words in your picture dictionary.  87

bike

boat

scooter

teddy bear

B Listen and color. 88

C Listen and write. 89

1. _____ boat _____

2. _____

3. _____

4. _____

Listen

LISTENING GOAL: Listen for Likes

Likes are things people think are good. Listen for likes to know how people feel about things.

A **Listen. Then complete the sentences.** 🔊 90

1. The girl likes the _____ball._____

2. The boy likes to ride on the _____

3. She likes the _____

Teddy Bear and Bird

B **Listen to the story *Teddy Bear and Bird*. What is it about? Choose the correct picture.** 🔊 91

A

B

Now put the sentences in order.

a. They go on a boat.   ☐

b. Teddy Bear rides a bike.   [1]

c. Bird flies up.   ☐

What does Bird **like**?

Think!

• What toys do you like?

Understand

A Think about **Teddy Bear and Bird**.
What does Teddy Bear like?

☐ a. the bike

☐ b. the scooter

> **Remember!**
> **Likes** tell how people
> feel about things.

B Listen to **Teddy Bear and Bird** again.
Choose the correct answer. 🔊 92

1. Teddy Bear has a **ball** / **balloon**.

2. The bike is **big** / **little**.

3. The scooter is **little** / **big**.

4. The boat is **old** / **fast**.

5. Bird **gets** / **doesn't get** the balloon.

C Listen. Complete each sentence with a key word. Then match. 🔊 93

1. I see a blue _____boat._____

2. He rides a _____

3. Is this your _____

4. She has a new _____

a. _____

b. _____

c. _1_

d. _____

D Listen to **Teddy Bear and Bird** again. What does Teddy Bear like? What does Bird like? Complete the diagram. 🔊 94

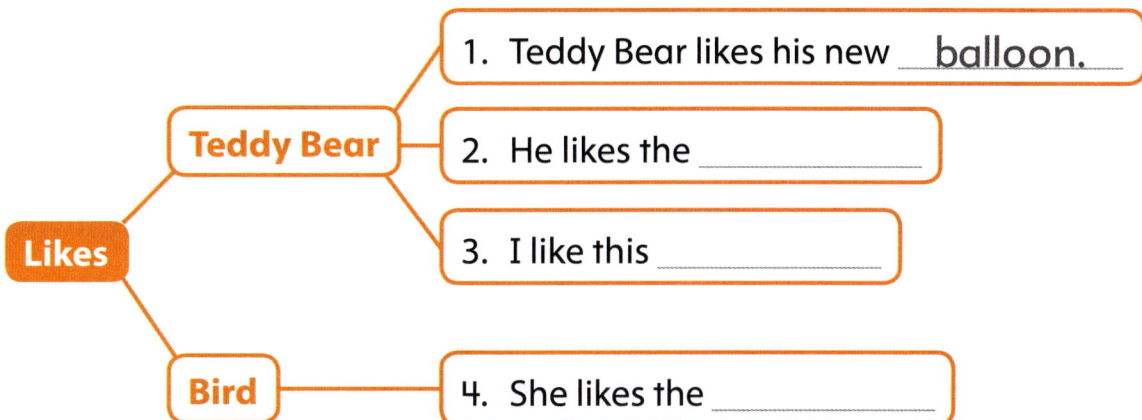

1. Teddy Bear likes his new ___balloon.___

Teddy Bear

2. He likes the _____

Likes

3. I like this _____

Bird

4. She likes the _____

E Look at **D**. Write. Use *like* or *likes*.

1.

He ___likes___ his new balloon.
It's fun!

2.

He _____ the bike.
It's big.

3.

"I _____ this boat," says
Teddy Bear.

4.

She _____ the scooter.
It's little.

MY LISTENING GOALS

☐ I can listen to the story.

☐ I can listen for likes.

Get Ready to Listen

Let's learn the **key words**.

A Listen, point, and say. Write the words in your picture dictionary. 95

carrots

mango

peach

tomato

B Listen and number. 96

C Listen and complete the sentences. 97

1. The ___carrots___ are on the table.

2. He eats the _____

3. I don't have a _____

4. Where is the _____

Listen

LISTENING GOAL: Listen for Dislikes

Dislikes are things people think are bad. Listen for dislikes to know how people feel about things.

A Listen. Is the picture correct? Choose ✔ or ✘. 98

1.

2.

3.

Pete and Mia

B Listen to the passage *Pete and Mia*. What is it about? Choose the correct picture. 🔊 99

A

B

Now choose ✔ or ✘.

1. Pete and Mia are thirsty.

2. Mia doesn't like the salad.

3. Pete and Mia have mango juice.

Does Mia **like** carrots?

Think!

• What foods do you like? What foods don't you like?

Understand

A **Think about Pete and Mia.**
What doesn't Mia like?
Choose the correct answer.

☐ a. fish   ☐ b. tomatoes

> **Remember!**
> People sometimes say
> what they **don't like**.
> Listen for these words.

B **Listen to Pete and Mia again. Choose the correct answer.** 🔊 100

1. What is in the salad?
   ☐ a. eggs   ☑ b. carrots
2. What does Mia like?
   ☐ a. peaches   ☐ b. pizza
3. How do Pete and Mia feel?
   ☐ a. sad   ☐ b. happy

C **Listen and choose the correct picture. Then write the key word.** 🔊 101

1.
☑ a.   ☐ b.

tomato

2.
☐ a.   ☐ b.

3.
☐ a.   ☐ b.

4.
☐ a.   ☐ b.

D Listen to **Pete and Mia** again. What doesn't Mia like? Complete the diagram. 🔊 102

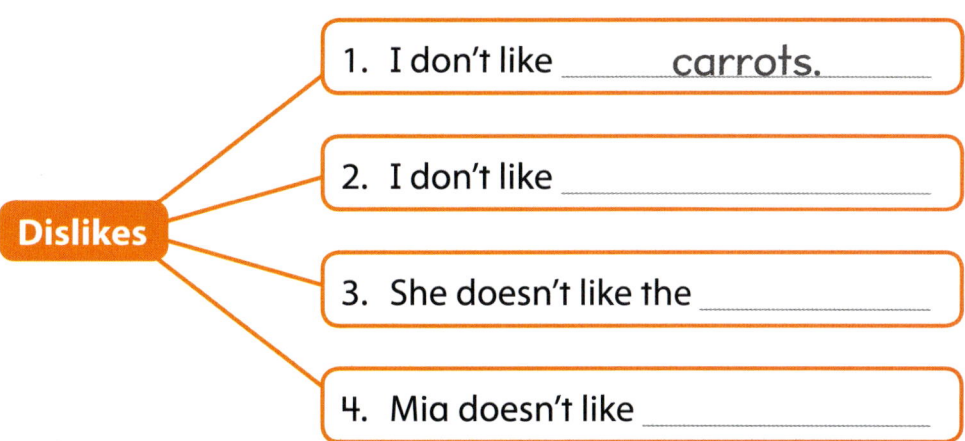

Dislikes

1. I don't like _____carrots._____

2. I don't like _____

3. She doesn't like the _____

4. Mia doesn't like _____

E Look at **D**. Write. Use *don't like* or *doesn't like*.

1.

I ___don't like___ carrots.

2.

I _____ tomatoes.

3.

She _____ the salad.

4.

Mia _____ mangoes.

MY LISTENING GOALS

☐ I can listen to the passage.

☐ I can listen for dislikes.

Listening Check

A **Listen to the story What Do You Like?
Choose the correct picture.** 🔊 103

A

B

C

B **What do Jake and Ben like? Choose ✔ or ✘.**

1. Jake likes bikes. ✔ ⊗
2. Jake likes carrots. ✔ ✘
3. Ben likes peaches. ✔ ✘
4. Ben likes chicken. ✔ ✘

C **What do Jake and Ben *not* like? Choose ✔ or ✘.**

1. Ben doesn't like scooters. ⊘ ✘
2. Jake doesn't like scooters. ✔ ✘
3. Ben doesn't like carrots. ✔ ✘
4. Jake doesn't like chicken. ✔ ✘

D Listen to **What Do You Like?** again. Choose the correct answer. 🔊 104

1. What do Jake and Ben do?
   - ☑ a. play
   - ☐ b. read
   - ☐ c. dance

2. Who has a scooter?
   - ☐ a. Jake
   - ☐ b. Ben
   - ☐ c. Lee

3. Who has a bike?
   - ☐ a. Jake
   - ☐ b. Ben
   - ☐ c. Lee

4. How do Jake and Ben feel?
   - ☐ a. sad
   - ☐ b. hungry
   - ☐ c. thirsty

5. What does Ben's mom have?
   - ☐ a. chicken
   - ☐ b. sandwiches
   - ☐ c. cake

E Listen to **What Do You Like?** again. Complete the sentences. 🔊 105

Jake and Ben play outdoors.

"I like my (1) ___scooter___ . It's fast!" says Jake.

But Ben doesn't like scooters.

They're little.

Ben likes (2) _____!

Jake and Ben are hungry.

"I like (3) _____," says Jake.

But Ben doesn't like carrots.

He likes (4) _____

"Boys!" says Ben's mom. "Do you want chicken?"

They like chicken! They go!

Get Ready to Speak

SPEAKING GOAL: Describe Likes and Dislikes
Likes are things you feel good about.
Dislikes are things you do not like.

A Read and listen to the conversation. Underline *and* and *but*.  106

> **Speaking Tip**
> Use *and* and *but* to talk about likes and dislikes.

Karam: I like video games, but I don't like books. What do you like?

Beth: I like puppets. Do you like fruit?

Karam: Yes, I like mangoes and bananas.

Beth: I like mangoes, but I don't like bananas.

B Look at **A**. What do Karam and Beth like? What don't they like? Complete the diagram.

Karam

Likes	Dislikes
1. video games	4. _____
2. _____	
3. _____	

Beth

Likes	Dislikes
5. _____	7. _____
6. _____	

Speak

C Think. What do you like? What don't you like? Complete the diagram.

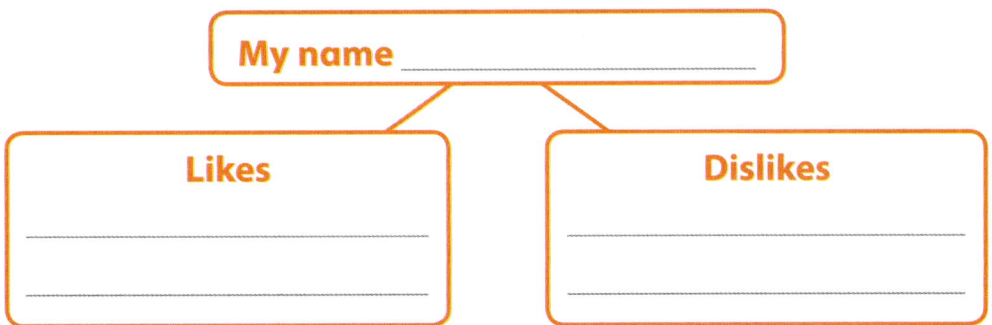

My name _____

Likes	Dislikes
_____	_____
_____	_____

D Now work with your partner. Write about your likes and dislikes. Use your ideas from **C**. Choose new words, too. Then draw one like and one dislike.

Me: I like _____, but I don't like

_____. What do you like?

My partner: I like _____.

Do you like _____?

Me: Yes, I like _____

and _____.

My partner: I like _____,

but I don't like _____.

 Say your conversation with your partner. Talk about your likes and dislikes.

MY SPEAKING GOAL

☐ I can talk about likes and dislikes.

My Face and Body

MY GOALS

UNIT 11

- Listen to the story *Tim Tiger and Friends*
- Listen for characters and names

UNIT 12

- Listen to the conversation *Funny Face*
- Listen for the speaker

SPEAK

- Describe a favorite activity

A Look at the picture. What do you see?

1. What can the girl do?
2. Do you do this? Do you like it? Why or why not?

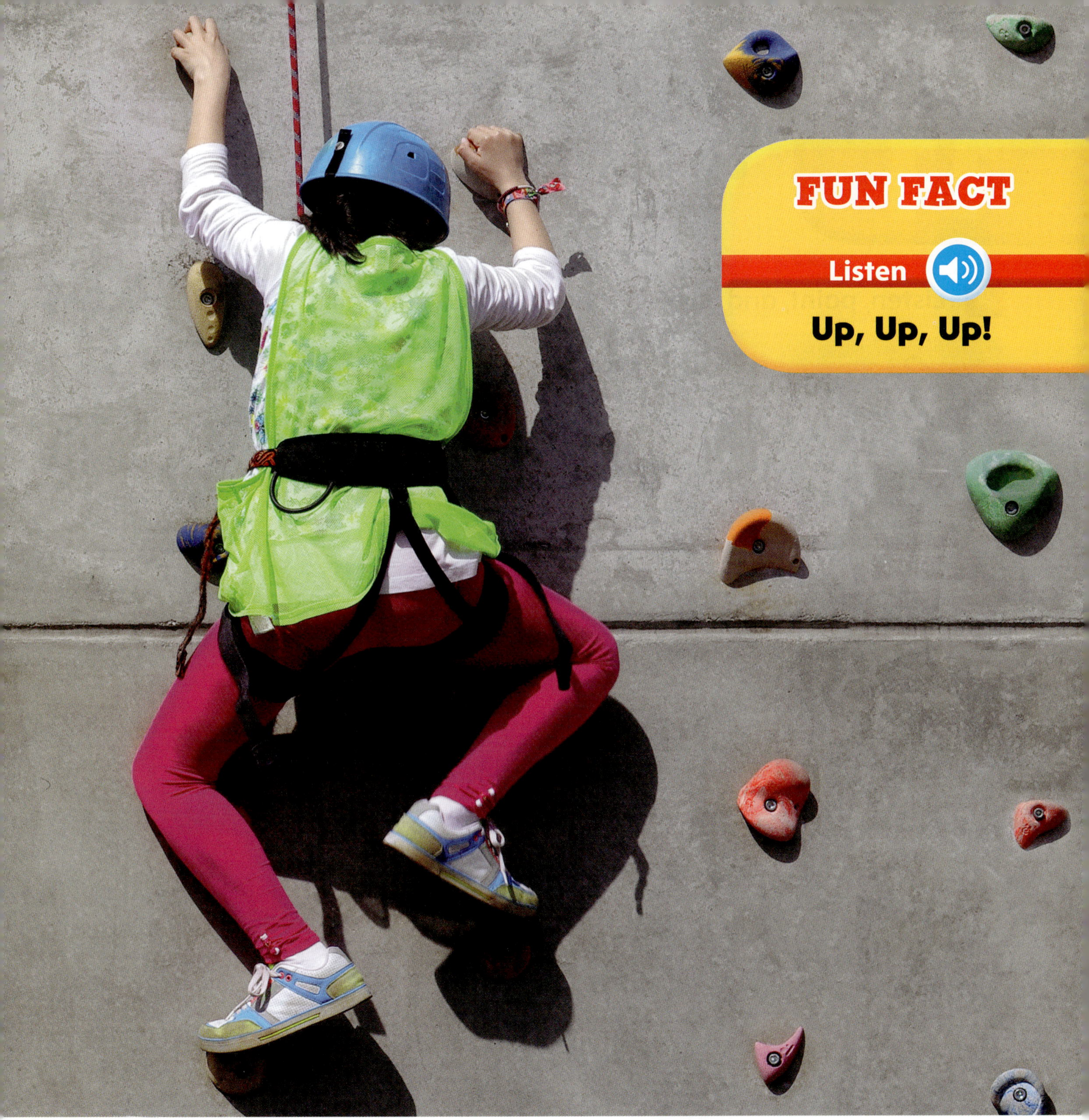

FUN FACT

Listen

Up, Up, Up!

B **Listen to the Fun Fact. Then answer the questions.** 107

1. What does the girl use to climb?
2. What can you do with your hands and feet?

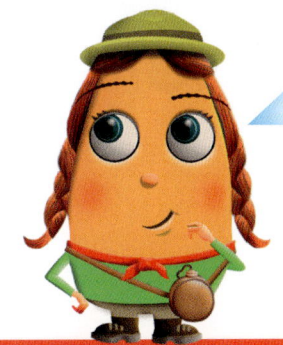

Think, Pair, Share
What do you like to do outdoors?

Get Ready to Listen

Let's learn the **key words**.

A Listen, point, and say. Write the words in your picture dictionary. 108

body

head

legs

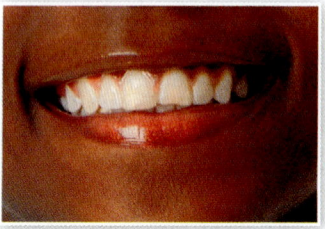

teeth

B Listen and color. 🔊 109

C Listen and write. 🔊 110

1. _____legs_____

2. _____

3. _____

4. _____

Listen

LISTENING GOAL: Listen for Characters and Names
Some stories are about people or animals. Listen for names of characters.
They tell who is in the story.

A Listen. Then complete the sentences. 🔊 111

1. ___Harry___ is a lion.

2. The two hands are _____'s.

3. The girl's name is _____

Tim Tiger and Friends

B Listen to the story *Tim Tiger and Friends*. What is it about?
Choose the correct picture. 🔊 112

A

B

Now put the sentences in order.

a. Tim Tiger is in the triangle. ☐

b. The mouse and the hen help. ☐

c. Tim Tiger jumps. ☐1

Who are the **characters**?

Think!

• Who are your favorite characters from stories?

Understand

A Think about **Tim Tiger and Friends**.
Who is in the story?

- ☐ a. Tim, Peter, and Max
- ☐ b. Tim, Max, and Heidi

> **Remember!**
> Listen for **names**. Names tell who the characters are.

B Listen to **Tim Tiger and Friends** again.
Choose the correct answer. 🔊 113

1. Tim Tiger has a big **arm** / (**head**).
2. He has long **legs** / **ears**.
3. The mouse has a **little** / **big** triangle.
4. Heidi pulls **Tim** / **Max**.
5. Tim Tiger has **little** / **big** teeth.

C Listen. Complete each sentence with a key word. Then match. 🔊 114

1. We have two ____legs.____
2. I brush my _____
3. I can touch my _____
4. This is my _____

a. ____

b. ____

c. ____

d. __1__

D Listen to **Tim Tiger and Friends** again. What does Tim Tiger have? Complete the table. 🔊 115

	long	big
1. head		✔
2. body		
3. legs		
4. teeth		

E Look at **D**. Complete the sentences. Use *long* or *big*.

1.

He has ___a big head.___

2.

He has _____

3.

He has _____

4.

He has _____

Get Ready to Listen

Let's learn the **key words**.

A Listen, point, and say. Write the words in your picture dictionary. 🔊 116

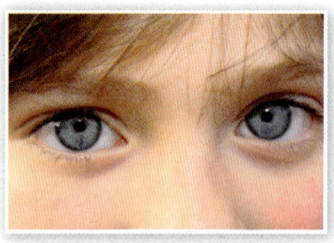  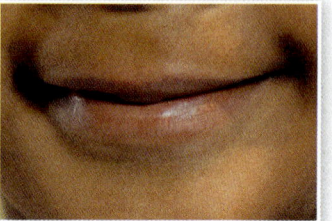 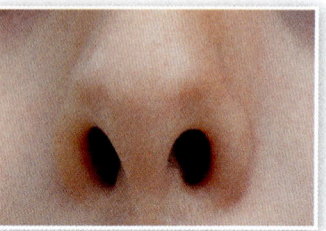

eyes   **face**   **mouth**   **nose**

B Listen and number. 🔊 117

C Listen and complete the sentences. 🔊 118

1. My ___face___ is little and round.

2. I can touch my _____

3. I have a long _____

4. This is my _____

Listen

LISTENING GOAL: Listen for the Speaker

The speaker is the person talking. There can be many speakers.
Names tell who the speakers are.

A Listen. Are the speakers' names correct? Choose ✔ or ✘. 🔊 119

1.  Sally
2. Cora Kenny
3. Julie Kazu

B Listen to the conversation *Funny Face*. What is it about?
Choose the correct picture. 🔊 120

 A

 B

Now choose ✔ or ✘.

1. Anna makes a pizza.
2. Mike helps.
3. They make a face.

*Who are the **speakers**?*

Think!

• What can you make with fruit?

Understand

A Think about **Funny Face**. Who are the speakers? Choose **Yes** or **No**.

1. Anna and Mike   **Yes**   **No**
2. Jacob and Anna   **Yes**   **No**

> **Remember!**
> Listen for **names**.
> Who speaks?

B Listen to **Funny Face** again. Choose the correct answer. 🔊 121

1. What does Anna have?
   - ☐ a. cherries
   - ☑ b. a banana
2. What does Mike have?
   - ☐ a. apples
   - ☐ b. cherries
3. What does Anna make?
   - ☐ a. a nose
   - ☐ b. eyes

C Listen and choose the correct picture. Then write the key word. 🔊 122

1. ☑ a.   ☐ b.

   _____ face _____

2. ☐ a.   ☐ b.

   _____

3. ☐ a.   ☐ b.

   _____

4. ☐ a.   ☐ b.

   _____

What can you do?

Anna
I can make

1. _____ a mouth _____

2. _____

Mike
I can make

3. _____

E Look and read. Write sentences. Use *can make*.

1.

FLOUR

What can she do?

_____ She can make a cake. _____

2.

What can she do?

_____

3.

What can she do?

_____

4.

What can she do?

_____

MY LISTENING GOALS

☐ I can listen to the conversation.

☐ I can listen for the speaker. The speaker is the person who talks.

Listening Check

A Listen to the story **What Is It?**
Choose the correct picture. 🔊 124

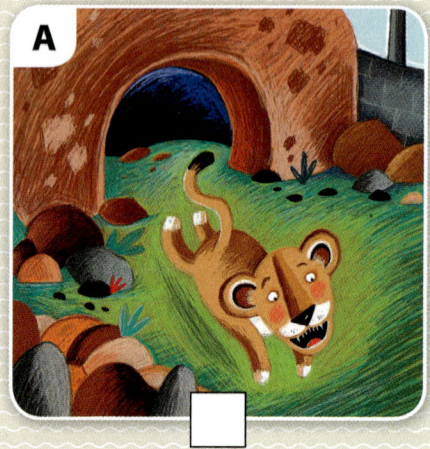

A

B

C

B Who are the characters? Choose ✔ or ✘.

1. Lucy   ✔   ✘
2. Emma   ✔   ✘
3. Shoma   ✔   ✘
4. Maya   ✔   ✘

C Listen to **What Is It?** again. Who is the speaker?
Choose the correct answer. 🔊 125

1. "I see something!"   Lucy   Shoma
2. "What is it?"   Lucy   Maya
3. "It has little teeth!"   Maya   Shoma
4. "It has short legs!"   Shoma   Maya

D Listen to **What Is It?** again. Choose the correct answer. 🔊 126

1. Where are the friends?

☐ a. at the park ☐ b. by the flowers ☑ c. at the zoo

2. What does the animal have?

☐ a. a big nose ☐ b. big teeth ☐ c. long legs

3. What does the animal have?

☐ a. round eyes ☐ b. blue eyes ☐ c. green eyes

4. What is the animal?

☐ a. a baby frog ☐ b. a baby bird ☐ c. a baby lion

5. What does the animal do?

☐ a. It runs. ☐ b. It jumps. ☐ c. It climbs.

E Listen to **What Is It?** again. Complete the sentences. 🔊 127

Lucy, Shoma, and Maya are at the zoo.

"I see something!" says Shoma.

"What is it?" asks Lucy.

"I don't know."

"It has a big (1) _____nose_____!" says Maya.

"It has little (2) _____!" says Shoma.

"It has round (3) _____!" says Lucy.

"It has short (4) _____!" says Maya.

It's a baby lion!

The lion jumps.

Get Ready to Speak

SPEAKING GOAL: Describe a Favorite Activity

An activity is something you do. You can give a description of an activity. You can say where you do it. You can also say how you feel about it.

A Read and listen to the passage **My Favorite Activity**. Underline *I'm* and *It's*. 🔊 128

> **Speaking Tip**
> *I am = I'm. It is = It's.* Use *I'm* and *It's* in your description about your activity.

My Favorite Activity

I like soccer. It's fun.

I play in the park. It's big.

I'm happy.

B Look at **A**. What does the speaker say? Complete the diagram.

What is it?

1. ___soccer___

My Favorite Activity

Where do you do it?

2. _____

How do you feel?

3. _____

Speak

C Think about your favorite activity. Complete the diagram.

What is it?
_____

My Favorite Activity

Where do you do it?
_____

How do you feel?
_____

D Now write about your favorite activity. Use your ideas from **C**. Choose new words, too. Then draw your activity.

I like _____.

It's _____.

I _____ in / at _____.

It's _____.

I'm _____.

 Talk about your favorite activity with your partner.

Oxford Skills World

Listening 1
with Speaking

Workbook

Julie Hwang

OXFORD
UNIVERSITY PRESS

WORKBOOK

UNIT 1

Listen

LISTENING GOAL:
Listen for the Title

Remember!
The **title** tells what the listening is about. It's at the beginning.

A Listen to the story **A Friend for Duck**. What is it about? Choose ✔ or ✗. 🔊 129

1. a duck and a mouse ☑✔ ☐✗

2. a duck and a cow ☑✔ ☐✗

B Think about **A Friend for Duck**. What does the title tell you about the story? Choose ✔ or ✗.

1. Duck wants a friend. ☑✔ ☐✗

2. Duck has a ball. ☑✔ ☐✗

3. There is an animal in the story. ☑✔ ☐✗

C Listen to **A Friend for Duck** again. Choose the correct answer. 🔊 130

1. Who helps Duck?
   ☐ a. Duck ☑ b. Cow ☐ c. Mouse

2. Where are the animals?
   ☐ a. at the park ☐ b. at the zoo ☐ c. at the farm

3. What does Duck see?
   ☐ a. a sheep ☐ b. a tree ☐ c. a bee

4. How many little ducks are there?
   ☐ a. 2 ☐ b. 10 ☐ c. 12

D Listen and write the word. Then choose the correct picture. 🔊 131

1. _____ duck _____

☐ a.   ✔ b.

2. _____

☐ a.   ☐ b.

3. _____

☐ a.   ☐ b.

4. _____

☐ a.   ☐ b.

E Complete the sentences.

| duck   sheep   ~~cow~~   monkey |

1. We drink milk from the _____ cow. _____

2. The _____ can climb.

3. A _____ can fly.

4. A _____ can eat grass all day.

F Unscramble and write.

1. k u d c

_____ duck _____

2. p h e s e

_____

3. o y e k m n

_____

4. o c w

_____

Listen

LISTENING GOAL:
Listen for the Topic

Remember!
The **topic** is what the listening is about. Look at the **title** and **pictures**. They can tell you the topic.

A Listen to the conversation **City Zoo**. Then put the pictures in order. 🔊 132

B Think about **City Zoo**. What is the topic? Choose ✔ or ✘.

1. Don has an apple. ✔ ✘

2. Amy and Don have fun at the zoo. ✔ ✘

3. The zoo is too big. ✔ ✘

C Listen to **City Zoo** again. Choose **Yes** or **No**. 133

1. Amy is hot.   **Yes**   **No**

2. There are seven crocodiles.   **Yes**   **No**

3. The elephant is under the tree.   **Yes**   **No**

4. Don and Amy see a giraffe.   **Yes**   **No**

5. Don is hungry.   **Yes**   **No**

6. There is a bee on the apple.   **Yes**   **No**

D Listen. Then read and choose the correct answer. 🔊 134

1. What does the girl see?

a.  b.  c.

2. What is at the zoo?

a.  b.  c.

3. What is old?

a.  b.  c.

E Complete the sentences.

1. The _____ elephant _____ is big.

2. The _m_____ is little.

3. The _g_____ is tall.

4. The _c_____ is very long.

Speak

Remember!
Use *I* and *my* to give
an introduction.

Circle *I* and *my*.

I am 7 years old.

Jean is my friend.

I like my new game.

Listen

LISTENING GOAL:
Listen for Numbers

A Listen to the conversation **A Robot**. What is it about?
Choose ✔ or ✘. 🔊 135

1.

a paper robot   ✔ ✘

2.

a book   ✔ ✘

B Think about **A Robot**. Are the numbers correct? Choose ✔ or ✘.

1. There is one heart.   ✔ ✘

2. There are two squares.   ✔ ✘

3. There are three rectangles.   ✔ ✘

C Listen to **A Robot** again. Choose the correct answer. 🔊 136

1. Who has paper?
   ✔ a. Min-Jun   ☐ b. Sue   ☐ c. Ella

2. What color are the squares?
   ☐ a. white   ☐ b. brown   ☐ c. gray

3. What color are the rectangles?
   ☐ a. gray   ☐ b. brown   ☐ c. purple

4. What color is the heart?
   ☐ a. orange   ☐ b. pink   ☐ c. purple

D Listen and write the word. Then choose the correct picture. 🔊 137

1. _____white_____

☑ a.　　☐ b.

2. _____

☐ a.　　☐ b.

3. _____

☐ a.　　☐ b.

4. _____

☐ a.　　☐ b.

E Complete the sentences.

| circle | brown | square | ~~white~~ |

1. The snow is _____white._____

2. The sun is a _____

3. This is a _____ crayon.

4. It's a _____ box.

F Unscramble and write.

1. n o r b w

_____brown_____

2. i h e w t

_____

3. e l i c r c

_____

4. r u s e q a

_____

Listen

LISTENING GOAL:
Listen for Colors

Remember!
Color words tell what color things are.

A Listen to the story **Ice Cream Juice**.
Then put the pictures in order. 🔊 138

A
1

B
[ ]

C
[ ]

B Think about **Ice Cream Juice**. What are the colors? Choose ✔ or ✗.

1. white, red, and blue   ✔ ✗

2. blue, red, and brown   ✔ ✗

3. red, blue, and green   ✔ ✗

C Listen to **Ice Cream Juice** again. Choose Yes or No. 🔊 139

1. It's cold today.   Yes   (No)

2. Kate has three blue scoops.   Yes   No

3. She has two red scoops.   Yes   No

4. Kate has orange juice.   Yes   No

5. She is hungry.   Yes   No

6. Yuki is at the park.   Yes   No

D Listen. Then read and choose the correct answer. 🔊 140

1. What color is the umbrella?

   a. 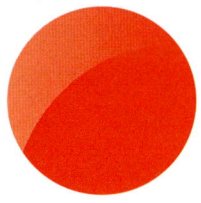   b.    (c.)

2. What color is the jump rope?

   a.    b. 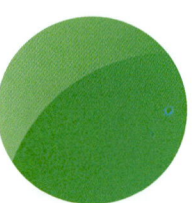   c.

3. What color is the kite?

   a.    b.    c.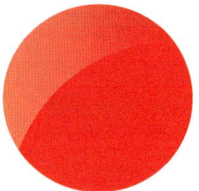

E Complete the sentences.

1. He has a _____blue_____ bicycle.

2. I have a y_____ pencil case.

3. The cup is g_____

4. I see a r_____ bird.

Speak

Remember!
Use color and shape words
in your description.

**What words tell about the robot? Circle them.
Then tell your partner.**

This is my robot. It's green.
It's little and new.

Listen

LISTENING GOAL:
Listen for Greetings and Endings

Remember!
Greetings start a conversation.
Endings stop a conversation.

A Listen to the story **Bob's Day**. What is it about? Choose ✔ or ✘. 🔊 141

1.

Bob has school. ✔ ✘

2.

Bob can play.

B Think about **Bob's Day**. What is the greeting? What is the ending? Choose ✔ or ✘.

1. hello and thank you ✔ ✘

2. hi and see you later ✔ ✘

3. hi and goodbye

C Listen to **Bob's Day** again. Choose the correct answer. 🔊 142

1. Where is the pen?
   - [✔] a. on the table
   - [ ] b. under the bed
   - [ ] c. on the chair

2. What does Bob look for?
   - [ ] a. a pencil
   - [ ] b. a notebook
   - [ ] c. glue

3. What does Bob think?
   - [ ] a. He is thirsty.
   - [ ] b. He is hungry.
   - [ ] c. He has school.

4. What day is it?
   - [ ] a. Sunday
   - [ ] b. Saturday
   - [ ] c. Friday

D Listen and write the word. Then choose the correct picture. 🔊 143

1. _____ notebook _____

☑ a.   ☐ b.

2. _____

☐ a.   ☐ b.

3. _____

☐ a.   ☐ b.

4. _____

☐ a.   ☐ b.

E Complete the sentences.

| notebook   pen   draw   eraser |

1. He writes in the _____ notebook. _____

2. I can _____ a picture.

3. She writes with a _____

4. The _____ is on the pencil.

F Unscramble and write.

1. e s a r e r

_____ eraser _____

2. n e p

_____

3. o e k b o n t o

_____

4. w a d r

_____

Listen

LISTENING GOAL:
Listen for Key Words

Remember!
You can hear some words many times. **Key words** tell what a listening is about.

A Listen to the presentation **My Picture**. Then put the pictures in order. 🔊 144

A

B

1

C

B Think about **My Picture**. What are the key words? Choose ✔ or ✗.

1. paint   ✔   ✗

2. scissors   ✔   ✗

3. paper   ✔   ✗

C Listen to **My Picture** again. Choose **Yes** or **No**. 145

1. The girl talks about a picture.   (Yes)   No

2. She is in the park.   Yes   No

3. The girl has paint.   Yes   No

4. She uses scissors.   Yes   No

5. The girl makes a circle.   Yes   No

6. The boys and girls take out paint.   Yes   No

D Listen. Then read and choose the correct answer. 🔊 146

1. What does the teacher have?

a.

b.

c.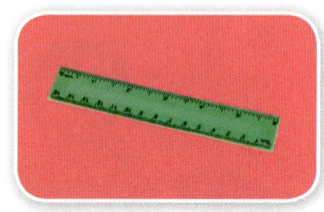

2. What is on the table?

a.

b.

c.

3. What is in the bag?

a.

b.

c.

E Complete the sentences.

1. He puts the pencil in the _____ backpack. _____

2. I use my r_____ to draw a square.

3. She goes to c_____

4. He writes on the p_____

Speak

> **Remember!**
> Use greetings like *hello* or *hi*. Use
> endings like *goodbye* or *see you later*.

Circle the greeting and the ending. Then think
of your own greeting and ending. Tell your partner.

"Hi, I'm Andrew."

"See you later!" says Jane.

Listen

LISTENING GOAL:
Listen for Questions

Remember!
Question words are words
like *what*, *where*, or *who*.
Questions ask for information.

A Listen to the story **The Snow Family**. What is it about?
Choose ✔ or ✘. 🔊 147

1.

a snowman   ✔ ✘

2.

my family   ✔ ✘

B Think about **The Snow Family**. What questions are in the story?
Choose ✔ or ✘.

1. What is this?   ✔ ✘

2. Who is the little girl?   ✔ ✘

3. Where is Sam?   ✔ ✘

C Listen to **The Snow Family** again. Choose the correct answer. 🔊 148

1. Who is Sam?
   ☐ a. a girl   ☐ b. a parent   ✔ c. a snowman

2. Who are they?
   ☐ a. Hugo's parents ☐ b. Sam's parents   ☐ c. Sam's friends

3. What does the girl do?
   ☐ a. kicks Sam   ☐ b. draws a square   ☐ c. climbs a tree

4. Where is Sam?
   ☐ a. at the farm   ☐ b. by the school   ☐ c. by the gate

D Listen and write the word. Then choose the correct picture. 🔊 149

1. _____children_____   2. _____

| ☐ a. | ✔ b. | ☐ a. | ☐ b. |

3. _____   4. _____

| ☐ a. | ☐ b. | ☐ a. | ☐ b. |

E Complete the sentences.

| children   boy   ~~parents~~   girl |

1. My _____parents_____ take me to school.

2. My brother is a _____

3. The _____ are in the playground.

4. The _____ has a yellow dress.

F Unscramble and write.

1. y o b

_____boy_____

3. l r e h i c n d

_____

2. e a r n p t s

_____

4. r i g l

_____

Listen

LISTENING GOAL:
Listen for Answers

Remember!
Answers come after questions. Listen for questions. Then listen for the answers.

A Listen to the conversation **Let's Play!**
Then put the pictures in order. 🔊 150

A

1

B

C

B Think about **Let's Play!** What answers are in the conversation?
Choose ✔ or ✘.

1. I play ball with Jenny.   ✔ ✘

2. She's my sister.   ✔ ✘

3. I go to the playground.   ✔ ✘

C Listen to **Let's Play!** again. Choose **Yes** or **No**. 🔊 151

1. Eva plays ball on Fridays.   **Yes**   **(No)**

2. Jenny is Eva's cousin.   **Yes**   **No**

3. They play at the park.   **Yes**   **No**

4. Eva has chicken.   **Yes**   **No**

5. Eva tells stories.   **Yes**   **No**

6. Jay flies a kite.   **Yes**   **No**

D Listen. Then read and choose the correct answer. 🔊 152

1. Who goes to the store?

   a.    b.    c.

2. Who likes plums?

   a.    b.    c.

3. Who has a red car?

   a.    b.    c.

E Complete the sentences.

1. My _____cousin_____ lives on a farm.

2. My u_____ is a teacher.

3. How many people are in your f_____?

4. My g_____ are 90 years old.

Speak

Circle the question words. Then think of your own questions. Tell your partner.

Who is she?

Where is this?

Remember!
Use question words. They are words like *who*, *what*, or *how*. They help you find information.

WORKBOOK
UNIT
9

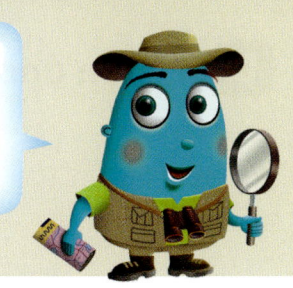

Listen

LISTENING GOAL:
Listen for Likes

Remember!
Likes are things we feel good about.

A Listen to the story Annie and the Toy. What is it about? Choose ✔ or ✘. 153

1. 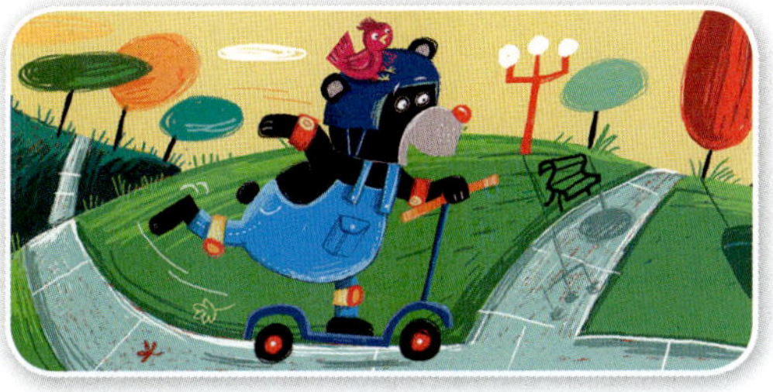

a bear on a scooter ✔ ✘

2. 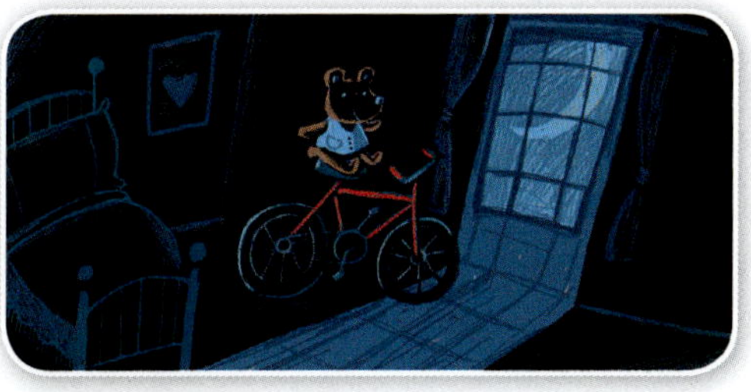

a teddy bear on a bike ✔ ✘

B Think about Annie and the Toy. What does Annie like? Choose ✔ or ✘.

1. the blue vest ✔ ✘
2. the scooter ✔ ✘
3. the teddy bear ✔ ✘

C Listen to Annie and the Toy again. Choose the correct answer. 154

1. Who is in bed?
   - ☐ a. a baby
   - ☐ b. Ted
   - ☑ c. Annie
2. What does Teddy Bear have?
   - ☐ a. a vest
   - ☐ b. a ball
   - ☐ c. a doll
3. Where does Annie look?
   - ☐ a. on the table
   - ☐ b. under the bed
   - ☐ c. in the box
4. Where is Teddy Bear?
   - ☐ a. on the car
   - ☐ b. on the book
   - ☐ c. on the bike

D Listen and write the word. Then choose the correct picture. 🔊 155

1. _____ bike _____

☑ a.   ☐ b.

2. _____

☐ a.   ☐ b.

3. _____

☐ a.   ☐ b.

4. _____

☐ a.   ☐ b.

E Complete the sentences.

~~teddy bear~~   boat   scooter   bike

1. I like my _____ teddy bear _____. It's little.

2. The _____ is in the water.

3. You stand up on a _____

4. Tom has a hat on his _____

F Unscramble and write.

1. r o t o c e s

_____ scooter _____

2. k i b e

_____

3. y e d t d r a b e

_____

4. a o t b

_____

Listen

LISTENING GOAL:
Listen for Dislikes

Remember!
Dislikes are things we don't feel good about.

A Listen to the passage **A Rainy Day**. Then put the pictures in order. 🔊 156

A [1]

B [ ]

C [ ]

B Think about **A Rainy Day**. What doesn't Eric like? Choose ✔ or ✘.

1. tomatoes   ✔ ✘
2. tomato juice   ✔ ✘
3. carrots   ✔ ✘

C Listen to **A Rainy Day** again. Choose ✔ or ✘. 🔊 157

1. Eric doesn't like rain.   ✘
2. He can go to the park.   ✔ ✘
3. Eric is thirsty.   ✔ ✘
4. He likes carrot cake.   ✔ ✘
5. He plays video games.   ✔ ✘
6. It's a bad day.   ✔ ✘

D Listen. Then read and choose the correct answer. 🔊 158

1. What does Rita want?

a.    b.   c.

2. What does he put in the box?

a.    b.    c.

3. What do they get?

a.    b.    c.

E Complete the sentences.

1. She makes a _____tomato_____ sandwich.

2. We can make _m_____ juice.

3. I can get a _p_____ from the tree.

4. The _c_____ are orange.

Speak

Remember!
We can use *and* and *but* to talk about likes and dislikes.

Circle *and* and *but*. Then think of your own sentences with *and* and *but*. Tell your partner.

I like cherries, and I like apples.

I like bananas, but I don't like banana bread.

Listen

LISTENING GOAL:
Listen for Characters and Names

Remember!
Listen for **names** of people or animals. They are the **characters**.

A Listen to the story **The Sisters**. What is it about? Choose ✔ or ✘. 🔊 159

1.

three girls   ✔ ✘

2.

two girls   ✔ ✘

B Think about **The Sisters**. Who are the characters? Choose ✔ or ✘.

1. Kay and Ella   ✔ ✘

2. Kay, Fran, and Ella   ✔ ✘

3. Kay, Fran, and Patty   ✔ ✘

C Listen to **The Sisters** again. Choose the correct answer. 🔊 160

1. What color is the house?
   ☑ a. blue   ☐ b. white   ☐ c. green

2. What can Kay do?
   ☐ a. sing   ☐ b. jump   ☐ c. dance

3. Who has red hair?
   ☐ a. the tall sister   ☐ b. the short sister   ☐ c. the baby

4. What can the baby do?
   ☐ a. jump   ☐ b. skip   ☐ c. stamp

Listen and write the word. Then choose the correct picture. 🔊 161

1. _____ legs _____

☑ a.   ☐ b.

2. _____

☐ a.   ☐ b.

3. _____

☐ a.   ☐ b.

4. _____

☐ a.   ☐ b.

E **Complete the sentences.**

| teeth | ~~body~~ | head | legs |

1. An elephant has a big _____ body. _____

2. The baby has two new _____

3. A mouse has short _____

4. Tom has a hat on his _____

F **Unscramble and write.**

1. e a d h

_____ head _____

2. h t e t e

_____

3. s l g e

_____

4. o d y b

_____

Listen

LISTENING GOAL:
Listen for the Speaker

Remember!
Listen for **names**.
They tell who the
speaker is.

A Listen to the interview **The Acrobat**.
Then put the pictures in order. 🔊 162

A

B

1

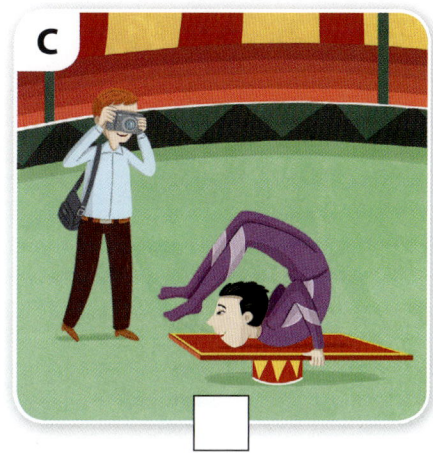

C

B Think about **The Acrobat**. Who are the speakers? Choose ✔ or ✘.

1. Henri   ✔   ✘

2. Ruby   ✔   ✘

3. Pierre   ✔   ✘

C Listen to **The Acrobat** again. Choose Yes or No. 🔊 163

1. Pierre can walk on his hands.   **(Yes)**   **No**

2. He can make a T with his body.   **Yes**   **No**

3. He can touch his eyes with his feet.   **Yes**   **No**

4. He can touch his nose with his knees.   **Yes**   **No**

5. Henri wants to draw a picture.   **Yes**   **No**

6. Henri is an acrobat.   **Yes**   **No**

D Listen. Then read and choose the correct answer. 🔊 164

1. What can she touch?

a. 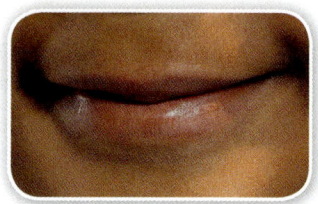   (b.)    c.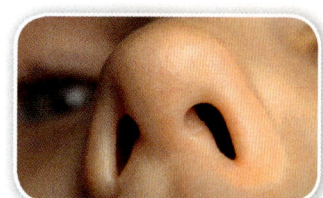

2. What is it?

a. 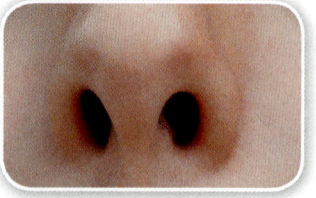   b. 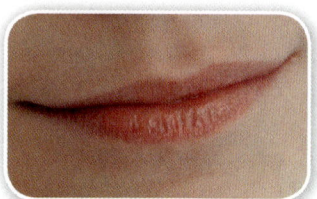   c.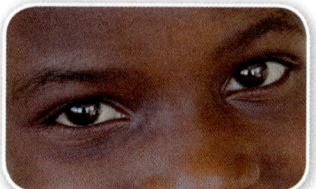

3. What is pretty?

a. 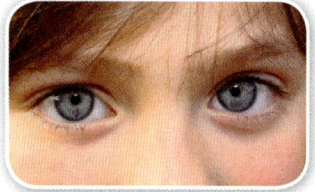   b.    c.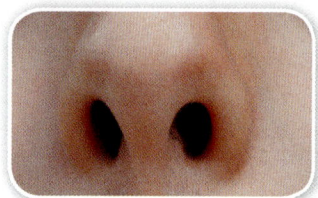

E Complete the sentences.

1. He has a round _____ face. _____

2. The tiger has a big m _____

3. Sunita has brown e _____

4. Ouch! I hurt my n _____

Speak

Circle *I'm* and *It's*. Then think of your own sentences with *I'm* and *It's*. Tell your partner.

I can play tennis. It's fun.

I play tag. I run and run. I'm hot.

Picture Dictionary

Write the key words.

Unit 1

Unit 3

Unit 2

Unit 4

Picture Dictionary

Unit 5

_____
_____
_____

_____
_____
_____

_____
_____
_____

_____
_____
_____

Unit 6

_____
_____
_____

_____
_____
_____

_____
_____
_____

_____
_____
_____

Unit 7

_____
_____
_____

_____
_____
_____

_____
_____
_____

_____
_____
_____

Unit 8

_____
_____
_____

_____
_____
_____

_____
_____
_____

_____
_____
_____

Unit 9

_____
_____
_____

_____
_____
_____

_____
_____
_____

_____
_____
_____

Unit 10

_____
_____
_____

_____
_____
_____

_____
_____
_____

_____
_____
_____

Unit 11

_____
_____
_____

_____
_____
_____

_____
_____
_____

_____
_____
_____

Unit 12

_____
_____
_____

_____
_____
_____

_____
_____
_____

_____
_____
_____

Syllabus

Topic	Unit	Listening Goal	Key Words	Speaking Goal
TOPIC 1 Animals Around Us	Unit 1	Listen for the title	*cow, duck, monkey, sheep*	Give an introduction
	Unit 2	Listen for the topic	*crocodile, elephant, giraffe, mouse*	Focus: *I* and *my*
TOPIC 2 Red Circle, Blue Square	Unit 3	Listen for numbers	*brown, circle, square, white*	Give a description
	Unit 4	Listen for colors	*blue, green, red, yellow*	Focus: Color and shape words
TOPIC 3 School Days	Unit 5	Listen for greetings and endings	*draw, eraser, notebook, pen*	Use greetings and endings
	Unit 6	Listen for key words	*backpack, class, paper, ruler*	Focus: Words to start and end conversations
TOPIC 4 Me and My Family	Unit 7	Listen for questions	*parents, boy, girl, children*	Ask questions to find information
	Unit 8	Listen for answers	*grandparents, uncle, cousin, family*	Focus: Question words
TOPIC 5 Likes and Dislikes	Unit 9	Listen for likes	*bike, boat, scooter, teddy bear*	Describe likes and dislikes
	Unit 10	Listen for dislikes	*carrots, mango, peach, tomato*	Focus: *And* and *but*
TOPIC 6 My Face and Body	Unit 11	Listen for characters and names	*body, head, legs, teeth*	Describe a favorite activity
	Unit 12	Listen for the speaker	*eyes, face, mouth, nose*	Focus: *I'm* and *It's*